BEST OF

Kraków

Richard Watkins

How to use this book

Colour-Coding & Maps

Each chapter has a colour code along the banner at the top of the page which is also used for text and symbols on maps (eg all venues reviewed in the Highlights chapter are orange on the maps). The fold-out maps inside the front and back covers are numbered from 1 to 6. All sights and venues in the text have map references; eg, (3, B3) means Map 3, grid reference B3. See p64 for map symbols.

Prices

Multiple prices listed with reviews (eg 10/6zł) usually indicate adult/concession admission to a venue. Concession prices can include senior, student, member or coupon discounts. Meal cost and room rate categories are listed at the start of the Eating and Sleeping chapters, respectively.

Text Symbols

- ☎ telephone
- ✉ address
- 💻 email/website address
- € admission
- ☺ opening hours
- ⓘ information
- Ⓜ metro
- 🚌 bus
- Ⓟ parking available
- ♿ wheelchair access
- ✗ on-site/nearby eatery
- child-friendly venue
- Ⓥ good vegetarian selection

Best of Kraków
1st edition – Jun 2006

Published by Lonely Planet Publications Pty Ltd
ABN 36 005 607 983

Australia Head Office, Locked Bag 1, Footscray, Vic 3011
☎ 03 8379 8000 fax 03 8379 8111
💻 talk2us@lonelyplanet.com.au
USA 150 Linden St, Oakland, CA 94607
☎ 510 893 8555 toll free 800 275 8555
fax 510 893 8572
💻 info@lonelyplanet.com
UK 72–82 Rosebery Avenue, London EC1R 4RW
☎ 020 7841 9000 fax 020 7841 9001
💻 go@lonelyplanet.co.uk

This title was commissioned in Lonely Planet's London office by Fiona Buchan and produced by Cambridge Publishing Management Limited. **Thanks** to Judith Bamber, Glenn Beanland, David Burnett, Steven Cann, Piotr Czajkowski, Brendan Dempsey, Jimi Ellis, Ryan Evans, Quentin Frayne, Jack Gavran, Michala Green, Mark Griffiths, Imogen Hall, Glenn van der Knijff, Marika Kozak, Charles Rawlings-Way, Michael Ruff, Wibowo Rusli, Fiona Siseman, Ray Thomson, Rachel Wood

Photographs by Lonely Planet Images and Kyzysztof Dydyński except for the following: p14 Photolibrary/Alamy, p25 Paul Springett/Alamy, p50 Photolibrary.

Cover photograph Siegfried Layda/Getty, St Mary's Church on Rynek Główny.

All images are copyright of the photographers unless otherwise indicated. Many of the images in this guide are available for licensing from Lonely Planet Images: www.lonelyplanetimages.com.

ISBN 1 74104 822 2

Printed through Colorcraft Ltd, Hong Kong.
Printed in China

Lonely Planet and the Lonely Planet logo are trademarks of Lonely Planet and are registered in the US Patent and Trademark Office and in other countries.

Lonely Planet does not allow its name or logo to be appropriated by commercial establishments, such as retailers, restaurants or hotels. Please let us know of any misuses: www.lonelyplanet.com/ip.

Although the authors and Lonely Planet have taken all reasonable care in preparing this book, we make no warranty about the accuracy or completeness of its content and, to the maximum extent permitted, disclaim all liability arising from its use.

Contents

From the Publisher

THE AUTHOR
Richard Watkins

After studying ancient history at Oxford, Richard's first job was teaching conversational English to college students in Bulgaria. He has since travelled the world, as an English teacher, backpacker and more recently as a travel guidebook author, and was very happy to spend some more time exploring his favourite Polish city in depth for this book. Richard was attracted back by Kraków's unique museums, imposing architecture, first-class restaurants and cosy, candle-lit subterranean pubs, while the fact that the city remains relatively free of the homogenised commercialism that has erupted elsewhere in the region is a bonus. Strolling through the golden-leafed Planty on a bright autumn morning, and sipping a cold beer on the Rynek as the notes of the *hejnał* drift from above, are among the Cracovian charms he hopes to experience again before too long. Richard has written for several other Lonely Planet titles, including *Poland*, *Eastern Europe* and *Best of Prague*.

LONELY PLANET AUTHORS

Why is our travel information the best in the world? It's simple: our authors are independent, dedicated travellers. They don't research using just the Internet or phone, and they don't take freebies in exchange for positive coverage. They travel widely, to all the popular spots and off the beaten track. They personally visit thousands of hotels, restaurants, cafés, bars, galleries, palaces, museums and more – and they take pride in getting all the details right, and telling it how it is. For more, see the authors section on **www.lonelyplanet.com**.

PHOTOGRAPHER
Krzysztof Dydyński

Born and raised in Warsaw, Poland, Krzysztof pretty early discovered a passion for worldwide travel, which took him on numerous trips to Asia and South America. In search of a new incarnation, in the early 1990s he made Australia his home; but, like a migratory bird, he has regularly returned to Poland, writing and photographing for Lonely Planet. Kraków is one of his great loves. He has been back time and again, revisiting his old secret corners and looking for new inspiration.

SEND US YOUR FEEDBACK

We love to hear from travellers – your comments keep us on our toes and help make our books better. Our well-travelled team reads every word on what you loved or loathed about this book. Although we cannot reply individually to postal submissions, we always guarantee that your feedback goes straight to the appropriate authors, in time for the next edition – and the most useful submissions are rewarded with a free book. To send us your updates – and find out about Lonely Planet events, newsletters and travel news – visit our award-winning website: **www.lonelyplanet.com/feedback**.

Note: We may edit, reproduce and incorporate your comments in Lonely Planet products such as guidebooks, websites and digital products, so let us know if you don't want your comments reproduced or your name acknowledged. For a copy of our privacy policy visit **www.lonelyplanet.com/privacy**.

Introducing Kraków

Poland's royal capital for 500 years and still the country's symbolic heart, Kraków is one of central Europe's loveliest cities. The remarkably well-preserved Old Town is a visual feast of Gothic, Renaissance and baroque architecture, the spires of myriad churches soaring high above quiet cobbled lanes and bustling shopping streets. Thankfully, the normally concrete-happy communist authorities left the city's historic centre well alone, and today more visitors than ever are coming to explore all that Kraków has to offer.

Kraków's origins go back as far as the 7th century, and its history has been tumultuous. Tatars, Teutonic Knights, Russians, Swedes, Austrians and Nazis all brought war and destruction over the centuries, while the city remained hidden behind the Iron Curtain for the four decades of totalitarian socialist rule.

Today, Kraków is a vibrant and cosmopolitan university city, though one that takes its cultural heritage and traditions very seriously. The home of Pope John Paul II is a deeply religious place; promenading monks, nuns and priests are a common sight, and you'll rarely come upon an empty church. The same can be said for Kraków's countless pubs and coffee bars, where sociable locals gather throughout the day. Visitors can also appreciate some of Poland's finest jazz acts and orchestral performances in this most cultured of cities.

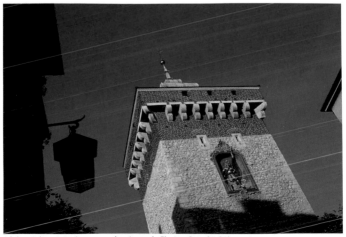

Of the eight original gates to the city, only Florian Gate (4, D2) survives

Neighbourhoods

Kraków is bisected by Poland's longest river, the Wisła, with the oldest and most interesting city districts being on the northern bank. The historic core of Kraków, and the hub of tourist activity, is the pleasingly compact **Stare Miasto** (Old Town), a vaguely oval area enclosed on the north, west and east sides by a strip of parkland called the **Planty** and bounded by Podzamcze in the south. It's centred on **Rynek Główny**, where you'll find the Cloth Hall and St Mary's Church, as well as a host of restaurants and shops. Many of Kraków's museums and churches, and

the best hotels, are also to be found in Stare Miasto.

To the south is **Wawel**, a small district consisting almost entirely of Wawel Hill, with its iconic castle and cathedral. Immediately to the east of Wawel is the equally tiny suburb of **Stradom**, home to a couple of churches, but of little interest to tourists.

South of Stradom is **Kazimierz**, the centre of Kraków's once thriving Jewish community. The main attraction here is the collection of synagogues, while the district is becoming a fashionable place for dining and drinking.

On the southern bank of the river, **Podgórze** was the site of the ghetto during WWII, and has a few more sights of Jewish interest, including the Schindler Factory.

Suburbs close to Stare Miasto include **Nowy Świat** to the west, home to the Filharmonia, National Museum and university departments, and the largely residential **Kleparz** to the north. More interesting is the 'socialist realist' suburb of **Nowa Huta**, 10km east, constructed in the 1950s for the workers at the mammoth on-site steelworks.

OFF THE BEATEN TRACK

Kraków can often seem besieged by hordes of visitors, but escaping the crowds is easy and involves no more than a short tram or bus ride.

Just 6km west of the centre, the vast woodland park of **Las Wolski** (p20) feels like an escape into the deepest countryside. Closer to hand, **Park Jordana** (p20) is another pleasant oasis of greenery where few tourists venture.

A visit to Mogiła's **Cistercian Monastery** (p18) can lead on to an exploration of the planned socialist suburb of **Nowa Huta** (p19), while the **Silesian House** (p18) and **Ethnographical Museum** (p14) are among the less-visited but still fascinating attractions.

For liquid refreshments with some local colour, try aptly named **Wódka** (p39) or vampire-themed **Transylwania** (p39).

Itineraries

Kraków is Poland's best-preserved medieval city, and the Old Town's wealth of historic buildings and monuments led to its being included in UNESCO's World Heritage list in 1978. More than six million visitors came to Kraków in 2004, making it by far Poland's most popular tourist destination.

Without a doubt, Wawel Castle is the main attraction for most visitors, while the numerous churches and museums and the Jewish legacy in Kazimierz also draw the crowds.

Many museums and galleries have free days, which are listed in the relevant reviews, while children and students, with valid ID, normally receive discounts. The Kraków Card (45/65zł for 2/3 days) provides unlimited transport around the city and access to around 30 museums, and can be bought at tourist offices and travel agencies.

Houses in Kazimierz, the Jewish quarter

DAY ONE

Make your first stop **Wawel Hill** (p8), with its magnificent castle and cathedral. From here, walk north to Stare Miasto and bustling **Rynek Główny** (p10). In the evening, try out one of the jazz clubs, or the opera at the **Słowacki Theatre** (p40).

DAY TWO

Take a tour around **Kazimierz** (p12), calling into the **Old Synagogue** (p19) and the excellent **Ethnographical Museum** (p14). While you're here, try some Jewish cuisine at **Klezmer Hois** (p35).

DAY THREE

Have an early start, with breakfast in **Metropolitan** (p32). Gaze at the awe-inspiring Veit Stoss Altar in **St Mary's Church** (p11), and explore the eclectic **Czartoryski Museum** (p13). Sample some traditional dumplings at **Pierogarnia** (p32) and round things off with a stroll through the **Planty** (p20).

WORST OF KRAKÓW
- Broken and uneven paving stones
- Winter smog
- Stuffy, smoke-filled pubs
- Pavement cyclists
- Huge flocks of fearless, low-flying pigeons in Rynek Główny

WAWEL HILL (5)

A precious symbol not just of Kraków, but of Poland itself, Wawel Hill is a place at the very heart of the nation's history. The castle here was the residence of Polish kings for 500 years, and even after the capital was transferred to Warsaw, they were still crowned, and buried, in the cathedral alongside.

INFORMATION

☎ 012 422 51 55

🖳 www.wawel.krakow.pl

✉ Wawel Hill

€ Royal Chambers 14/8zł, free Mon; Royal Private Apartments 18/13zł; Treasury & Armoury 14/8zł, free Mon; Museum of Oriental Art 6/4zł, free Mon; Lost Wawel 6/4zł, free Mon; Wawel Cathedral free; Royal Crypts & Sigismund Tower 10/5zł; Cathedral Museum 5/2zł; Dragon's Cave 3zł

⊙ Royal Chambers, Treasury & Armoury and Museum of Oriental Art 9.30am-noon Mon, 9.30am-4pm Tue & Fri, 9.30am-3pm Wed, Thu & Sat, 10am-3pm Sun Apr-Oct; Royal Private Apartments 9.30am-4pm Tue & Fri, 9.30am-3pm Wed, Thu & Sat, 10am-3pm Sun Apr-Oct; Lost Wawel 9.30am-4pm Tue & Fri, 9.30am-3pm Wed, Thu & Sat, 10am-3pm Sun Apr-Oct; Cathedral 9am-3.45pm Mon-Sat, 12.15-3.45pm Sun Apr-Oct; Cathedral Museum 10am-3pm Tue-Sun Apr-Oct; Dragon's Cave 10am-5pm Apr-Oct. Opening times for all museums Nov-Mar vary

ⓘ all tickets are for entry at specific times 🚌 103, 502

♿ fair (grounds, Cathedral, Lost Wawel, Museum of Oriental Art, Treasury & Armoury)

✕ on-site cafés

The first fortress on the hill was built in the 11th century but the present castle dates largely from the 16th century. Additions were made in the 19th century to accommodate the Austrian garrison.

Today, the castle houses several museums, the most impressive being the **Royal Chambers**. Here you can wander through a series of imposing rooms restored to their Renaissance-era splendour and filled with antique furnishings and art. The Senators' Hall, decorated with huge tapestries, and the Throne Hall, with its unique coffered ceiling, are particularly grand. The **Royal Private Apartments** offer a more intimate look at how the Polish royal family lived, with a guided tour through yet more sumptuous interiors.

The prize possession of the **Treasury & Armoury** is the *Szczerbiec* (Jagged Sword) which was used at all Polish coronations from 1320

Wawel Cathedral, the spiritual heart of the nation

onwards, and there's an extensive display of other medieval weaponry. Nearby, the **Museum of Oriental Art** features a collection of Turkish banners and weapons captured after the 1683 Battle of Vienna, as well as Chinese and Japanese ceramics.

The final castle museum, called the **Lost Wawel**, offers a glimpse of medieval Wawel and the remnants of the 10th-century Rotunda of SS Felix and Adauctus, reputedly the first church in Poland. There's also a display of archaeological finds from the site.

Wawel Cathedral is Poland's most important church, and walking around the numerous royal sarcophagi is like a tour through Polish history itself. This is the third church to stand on this site, and was completed in 1364. Among the many chapels, the showpiece is the Renaissance **Sigismund Chapel**, easily recognised from the outside by its gilded half-dome. It houses the red marble tombs of King Zygmunt I and his son, Zygmunt II.

THE WAWEL DRAGON
Wawel Hill was once terrorised by a dragon, and in good fairy-tale fashion, the king offered his daughter's hand to anyone who vanquished it. One plucky youth left a sheepskin filled with sulphur for the dragon. The dragon's stomach burned so much when he ate it that he rushed to the river and drank until he exploded.

None of the royal tombs, though, achieves the flamboyance of the baroque silver **Shrine of St Stanislaus** in the centre of the cathedral. Stanislaus, Poland's patron saint, was Archbishop of Kraków, until a spot of church–state friction got him beheaded in 1079.

The **Chapel of Queen Zofia**, to the left of the main entrance, is another highlight. Its beautiful stained glass and colourful murals are in the art nouveau style.

Ascend the **Sigismund Tower** to see the great Sigismund Bell, cast in 1520. At 2m high and weighing 11 tonnes, it's the largest historic bell in Poland. The 70 wooden steps are a bit of a squeeze in places.

Back down in the church, the tiny Poets' Crypt contains three tombs, including that of Adam Mickiewicz, the Romantic poet, while the dank **Royal Crypts** house the sarcophagi of several kings and national heroes such as Tadeusz Kościuszko and Józef Piłsudski.

Opposite the cathedral is the **Cathedral Museum**, which displays various ecclesiastical treasures and royal funerary regalia.

Complete your Wawel tour with a visit to the **Dragon's Cave**, one-time home to the legendary fire-breather. Once you buy your ticket from the machine outside, you descend 135 steps through the cave, emerging on the bank of the Wisła below.

RYNEK GŁÓWNY (2, A2)

Kraków's great medieval market square, measuring 200m by 200m, is the largest in Poland, and reputedly in all of Europe. It was originally laid out in 1257, and although many buildings have come and gone since then, the square itself has remained constant and is still the social and commercial hub of the Old Town.

At the centre of the square is the magnificent **Cloth Hall** (2, B2), built in the 14th century for, unsurprisingly, cloth merchants. It was remodelled in Renaissance style after a 1555 fire; today the ground level is still a busy centre of trade, with dozens of stalls selling amber, craftwork, T-shirts and other souvenirs to tourists. Upstairs, the **Cloth Hall Gallery** (p16) has the city's finest collection of Polish art.

Nearby, the tiny **St Adalbert's Church** (2, B3) is one of the oldest in Kraków, with foundations going back to the 10th century. Just north of this church is the **statue of Adam Mickiewicz** (2, B2), the 19th-century Romantic poet. This is where the *Szopki competition* (p50) is held each December.

Dominating the northeastern corner of the square is **St Mary's Church** (p11) while to the west of the Cloth Hall stands the **Town Hall Tower** (p20).

Rynek Główny is regularly used as a venue for open-air concerts and civic ceremonies of various kinds, and is lined on all sides with restaurants, bars, shops and banks, ensuring that this is one historic town square that isn't just a picturesque museum piece.

INFORMATION

- ⊠ Rynek Główny
- ⓘ tourist information office in Cloth Hall
- ♿ excellent
- ✕ Wierzynek (p31)

DON'T MISS
- The view from the Town Hall Tower
- Browsing the souvenir stalls in the Cloth Hall
- Having a drink at one of the outdoor cafés in the square
- Listening to the buskers

ST MARY'S CHURCH (2, C2)

Rising majestically over the northeastern corner of Rynek Główny, St Mary's is Kraków's most important church, after Wawel Cathedral. The original church, built in the 1220s, was destroyed during the Tatar raids, and the edifice you see today is a 15th-century creation. From the outside, the most striking feature of the church is its two towers, of unequal height.

According to one typically bloody legend, this was the result of a feud between two architect brothers, who had each been commissioned to build one tower and wanted to outdo each other. This competition ended with one knifing the other to death and then killing himself out of remorse. The less dramatic truth, though, is that the 69m-high tower was built to hold the church bells, while the other, 81m-high tower functioned as a city watchtower

Inside, the focus, for worshippers and tourists alike, is the magnificent **Veit Stoss Altar**, regarded as Poland's greatest masterpiece of Gothic art. Measuring around 13m high and 11m wide, this polychrome oak and lime pentaptych was created by the Nuremburg sculptor Veit Stoss, known in Poland as Wit Stwosz, between 1477 and 1489.

At the centre of the opened altarpiece, the largest of its kind in Europe, is a wonderfully expressive representation of the Assumption, while six panels (three on each side) recount episodes from the life of the Virgin Mary.

Other high points include the carved panels over the choir stalls and the nearby stone crucifix, also by Stoss.

INFORMATION

☎ 012 422 05 21
✉ Rynek Główny 4
€ 4/2zł
☾ 11.30am-6pm Mon-Sat,
  2-6pm Sun
ℹ ceremonial opening of the altar
  at 11.50am
♿ good
✗ Szara (p30)

TRUMPETS & TATARS

Every hour the *hejnał* (bugle call) is played from the high tower of St Mary's Church. This medieval warning call stops abruptly in mid-bar. Legend says that a 13th-century watchman was felled by a Tatar arrow in the middle of his bugling, and the tune has remained this way in his memory.

KAZIMIERZ (6)

Today one of Kraków's inner suburbs, Kazimierz was once an independent town, founded by, and named after, King Kazimierz Wielki in 1335. Jews settled here in large numbers after they were expelled from Kraków in 1494, while Poles continued to live in their own 'Christian quarter'.

INFORMATION
- ☎ 012 430 64 49 (Judaica Foundation)
- ✉ Judaica Foundation, Meiselsa 17
- ⓘ guided tours available from Jarden Tourist Agency (p25)
- 🚋 3, 6, 8, 9, 10, 11, 13, 24
- ♿ good (some cobbles/rough ground)
- 🍴 Klezmer Hois (p35)

DON'T MISS
- The exhibition at the Galicia Jewish Museum (p16)
- Tasting Jewish caviar and kosher vodka at Klezmer Hois or Arka Noega (p35)
- The Renaissance tombstones in Remuh Cemetery (p19)
- The art exhibitions at the Judaica Foundation (6, B2)
- The market on Plac Nowy (6, B2)

Kazimierz was incorporated into the city of Kraków in 1791, ending its administrative independence. By the beginning of the 20th century, Kazimierz was a largely Jewish neighbourhood, although by this time only the poorest Jews remained. The Nazis herded the Jews into a ghetto in Podgórze, across the river, before transporting them to Auschwitz and elsewhere to be murdered.

Today only two of Kazimierz's synagogues are still in use by Kraków's tiny Jewish population; the Orthodox **Remuh Synagogue** (p19) and the Reform **Tempel Synagogue** (p19). Others, such as the **Old Synagogue** (p19) and **Isaac's Synagogue** (p19), now function as museums. Meanwhile the **Judaica Foundation** (6, B2) hosts exhibitions on Jewish themes.

Although it still has its shabby and derelict areas, Kazimierz today is a lively place, full of fashionable restaurants and bars. The heart of the quarter is Szeroka, a broad street lined with several restaurants offering Jewish-inspired cuisine, as well as a couple of hotels. This is also the main venue for the annual **Jewish Cultural Festival** (p41).

Southwest of here is the **Corpus Christi Church** (Bożego Ciała 26), built in 1340. Its spacious baroque interior is worth a visit for its impressive altar, boat-shaped pulpit and 15th-century stained-glass windows.

CZARTORYSKI MUSEUM (4, D2)

This varied and endlessly intriguing museum was originally established in 1800 by Princess Izabela Czartoryska, in the eastern Polish town of Puławy. In 1870 the collection was transferred to Kraków, and, apart from an excursion to Nazi Germany during WWII, it has been here ever since.

Among the first exhibits to greet visitors are an assemblage of Turkish weaponry, armour, saddles and rugs and a campaign tent recovered after the 1683 Battle of Vienna. Also on display are exquisite pieces of Meissen porcelain and some fine glassware. Some of the museum's most fascinating treasures are in the archaeology gallery. Mummified birds from ancient Egypt, Etruscan sarcophagi, Babylonian cylinder seals, Greek vases and Roman statues are among the remarkably rich array of artefacts.

Other oddities on this floor include a tricorn hat which belonged to the last king of Poland, Stanisław August Poniatowski, and Frederic Chopin's death-mask. It's the art gallery upstairs, though, that's the main draw.

Displayed in its own room, Leonardo da Vinci's stunning *Lady with an Ermine* (c1482) is Poland's most famous foreign painting. It is thought to represent a mistress of Duke Ludovico Sforza of Milan. Rembrandt's *Landscape with the Good Samaritan* (1638) is another highlight, while other standouts include *The Preaching of St John the Baptist* by Pieter Breughel the Younger and works by Bernardo Daddi and Lorenzo Monaco.

INFORMATION

- ☎ 012 422 55 66
- 🖳 www.muzeum-czartoryskich.krakow.pl
- ✉ Św Jana 19
- € 9/6zł, free Thu
- 🕙 10am-3.30pm Tue & Thu, 10am-6.30pm Wed, Fri & Sat, 10am-2.30pm Sun
- 🚊 2, 3, 4, 5, 13, 14
- 🍴 Farina (p31)

DON'T MISS

- Roman sleeping nymph statue
- Etruscan votive heads
- Tommaso di Stefano's *Adoration of the Shepherds*
- Turkish sultan's chess set

ETHNOGRAPHICAL MUSEUM (6, B3)

Built in the late 14th century, this grand building, with its Renaissance façade, was once the town hall of Kazimierz (p12), and today houses an extensive exhibition on Polish folk traditions and customs. It's an absorbing museum with a huge and varied collection, although one which sees far fewer visitors than it rightly deserves.

INFORMATION

☎ 012 430 55 63
✉ Plac Wolnica 1, Kazimierz
€ 6.50/4zł, free Sun
⏰ 10am-5pm Mon & Wed-Fri, 10am-2pm Sat & Sun May-Sep, 10am-6pm Mon, 10am-3pm Wed-Fri, 10am-2pm Sat & Sun Oct-Apr
🚋 6, 8, 10
🍴 Kuchnia i Wino (p35)

SPRING RITES

Seasonal rituals were an intrinsic part of rural life in Poland. To herald each new spring, a straw doll, personifying winter, was dressed in women's clothes and symbolically burned and 'drowned'. Then, a decorated tree, called a *gaik*, would be paraded into the village, symbolising the arrival of the new season.

The displays begin on the ground floor with a collection of scale-model cottages showing different regional designs, but more immediately engaging are the full-size reconstructions of peasant cottage interiors, with their painted wooden ceilings, rustic furniture and stoves. There's also a reconstructed cloth workshop, with original wooden apparatus brought from a nearby mountain village, and an oil press, from Zakopane, in southern Poland.

Upstairs you can look over a gallery full of regional costumes and an exhibition on peasant community life, covering areas such as weddings and funerals, education, agriculture, cheese-making and bee-keeping. There's a reconstructed blacksmith's forge; and all the tools necessary for an often tough, self-sufficient rural existence such as ploughs, looms and spinning-wheels, as well as musical instruments.

Further displays illustrate the colourful festivals celebrated by country folk, including costumes worn by Christmas carollers, and the various rites associated with the coming of spring, plus a collection of painted Easter eggs from across the country.

Woodcuts, icons and religious carvings can be seen on the second floor, along with some amazing painted wooden beehives in the form of life-size figures of St Francis and St Ambrose and, appropriately, of a bear, among others.

COLLEGIUM MAIUS (4, B3)

Kraków's Jagiellonian University is one of the oldest in Europe, founded in 1364, and the Collegium Maius, dating from the 15th century, is Poland's oldest university building. Over the centuries it has undergone many renovations, and was much damaged during the Nazi occupation in the 1940s. However, since then it has been restored to something approaching its former glory, and is open to visitors.

The elegant arcaded court-yard is free to visit at any time, and is a highlight in itself. Look out for the clock, which chimes the old student song *Gaudeamus Igitur* at 1pm, as little figures troop past. If you wish to see the interior, though, you'll need to join one of the regular guided tours.

COPERNICUS
Nicolaus Copernicus, or, to give him his Polish name, Mikołaj Kopernik, studied at the Kraków Academy, now known as the Jagiellonian University, between 1491 and 1495. He postulated the 'heliocentric theory', that the Earth and other planets orbit the Sun, and not the other way round, as was then thought.

Inside, you can view treasures such as rare 16th-century astronomical instruments, supposedly used by the university's illustrious alumnus, Nicolaus Copernicus. Also here is a collection of rectors' sceptres and the world's oldest existing globe, showing the recently discovered continent of America, dated to 1510.

You will also visit the impressive *Aula*, a grand hall with an original Renaissance ceiling, full of portraits of kings, professors and university benefactors. This room is still used for ceremonial occasions.

On the ground floor there's an interactive exhibition hall, **Ancient & Modern Sciences**, which has hands-on displays and experiments covering subjects such as acoustic waves and alchemy, which scientifically minded kids might enjoy.

INFORMATION
- ☎ 012 422 05 49
- ✉ Jagiellońska 15
- € Museum 12/6zł; Ancient and Modern Sciences 6/4zł; courtyard free
- ☾ Museum 10am-3pm Mon-Wed & Fri, 10am-6pm Thu, 10am-2pm Sat; Ancient and Modern Sciences 10am-2.30pm Mon-Sat; courtyard 7am-sunset
- ⓘ tours must be reserved in advance
- 🚊 2, 7, 8, 15
- ♿ fair (courtyard only)
- ✕ on-site café

Sights & Activities

MUSEUMS & GALLERIES

Archaeological Museum (4, B5)

Małopolska's history from the Palaeolithic to the Middle Ages is chronicled with displays of locally excavated artefacts. There's also a fascinating exhibition of Egyptian antiquities, and a picturesque garden.
☎ 012 422 75 60
✉ Poselska 3 € 7/5zł
⏲ 9am-2pm Mon-Wed, 2-6pm Thu, 10am-2pm Fri & Sun 🚌 103, 502

Archdiocesan Museum (4, C6)

This grand building was once home to the late Pope John Paul II, when he was Archbishop of Kraków. Medieval religious art is on display, as well as some of the pontiff's personal belongings.
☎ 012 421 89 63
✉ Kanonicza 19 € 5/3zł

⏲ 10am-4pm Tue-Fri, 10am-3pm Sat & Sun
🚌 103, 502

Bunkier Sztuki (4, B2)

The ugly concrete 'bunker' is a leading gallery for temporary exhibitions of contemporary art. Paintings, sculptures and installations by both Polish and foreign artists are shown.
☎ 012 422 10 52 🖳 www.bunkier.com.pl ✉ Plac Szczepański 3 (entry on Planty) € 6/3zł ⏲ 11am-6pm Tue-Sun 🚋 2, 4, 7, 13, 14 ♿ fair (ground floor)

Cloth Hall Gallery (2, B2)

On the upper floor of the old market hall, this gallery hosts an impressive collection of 19th-century Polish paintings and sculptures, including several huge canvasses by Jan Matejko. His *Prussian Tribute in 1525* depicts an event that was staged on the square below.
☎ 012 422 11 66 🖳 www.

zpap.krakow.pl ✉ Rynek Główny 1 € 8/5zł, free Thu ⏲ 10am-7pm Tue, Fri & Sat, 10am-4pm Wed & Thu, 10am-3pm Sun May-Oct, 10am-3.30pm Tue, Thu, Sat & Sun, 10am-6pm Wed & Fri Nov-Apr

Eagle Pharmacy (3, D5)

This pharmacy once served the needs of the Jews herded into the Podgórze ghetto by the Nazis. It's now a museum dedicated to the harsh life of that ghetto.
☎ 012 656 56 25
✉ Plac Bohaterów Getta 18, Podgórze € 4/3zł
⏲ 10am-2pm Mon, 9.30am-5pm Tue-Sat May-Oct, 9am-4pm Tue-Thu & Sat, 10am-5pm Fri Nov-Apr
🚋 3, 9, 11, 13, 24

Galicia Jewish Museum (6, C2)

This gallery pays tribute to Poland's lost Jewish communities with a poignant exhibition of photographs documenting ruined synagogues and former Jewish neighbourhoods. There's a bookshop and a regular programme of events.
☎ 012 421 68 42 🖳 www.galiciajewishmuseum.org
✉ Dajwór 18, Kazimierz
€ 7/5zł ⏲ 9am-7pm
🚋 3, 9, 11, 13, 24
♿ excellent (all ground level)

Hipolit House (2, C2)

Also known as the Burgher House, this museum is dedicated to domestic history, with reconstructed interiors of middle-class homes from the 17th to the 20th centuries.
☎ 012 422 42 19 🖳 www.mhk.pl ✉ Plac Mariacki 3

Quiet contemplation in the Cloth Hall Gallery

€ 5/3zł, free Sat 🕐 10am-5.30pm Wed-Sun May-Oct, 9am-4pm Wed & Fri-Sun, noon-7pm Thu Nov-Apr

Historical Museum (2, A1)

Kraków's history from the Middle Ages through to WWII is presented here. Guild paraphernalia, charters, militia uniforms and armour are on display, as well as a roomful of mementos of the local revolutionary hero Tadeusz Kościuszko.

☎ 012 422 15 04 🖳 www.mhk.pl ✉ Rynek Główny 35 € 5/3zł, free Sat 🕐 10am-5pm Wed-Sun May-Oct, 9am-4pm Wed, 10am-5pm Thu-Sun Nov-Apr 🕭 fair (ground floor)

Jan Matejko House (4, D2)

The 19th-century artist Jan Matejko was born, and died, in this house, which now presents an exhibition on his life and works. Some of his most famous paintings can be seen in the Cloth Hall Gallery (p16).

☎ 012 422 59 26 🖳 www.muzeum.krakow.pl ✉ Floriańska 41 € 6/4zł, free Thu 🕐 10am-7pm Tue, Wed

Sample Japanese art, film and food at the Manggha Centre

& Sat, 10am-4pm Thu & Fri, 10am-3pm Sun May-Oct, 10am-3.30pm Wed, Thu, Sat & Sun, 10am-6pm Fri Nov-Apr

Manggha Centre of Japanese Art & Technology (3, C5)

This striking building on the south bank of the Wisła hosts a display of Japanese art including 19th-century bronzes, ceramics, silk paintings, kimonos and swords. Temporary exhibitions cover aspects of Japanese culture, and there's an on-site Japanese café (p36).

☎ 012 267 27 03 🖳 www.manggha.krakow.pl ✉ Konopnickiej 26 € 5/3zł, free Sun 🕐 10am-5.30pm Tue-Sun 🚌 114, 124, 144, 164, 179 🕭 good

National Museum (3, B4)

This boxy affair west of the city centre houses three permanent galleries showing 20th-century Polish paintings, decorative arts and weaponry. There are regular temporary exhibitions too.

☎ 012 295 55 00 ✉ Aleja 3 Maja 1, Zwierzyniec € 9/6zł 🕐 10am-4pm Tue & Wed, 10am-7pm Thu-Sat, 10am-3pm Sun 🚋 15, 18

Polish Aviation Museum (3, off F3)

Poland's largest collection of flying machines is displayed

MIND THOSE MOUNDS

Some of the more curious features of Kraków are its four earthwork mounds. **Krak's Mound** in Podgórze (3, E6), is 16m high and dates from the 7th century. According to legend, it's the tomb of Kraków's founder, King Krak, although its exact purpose remains a mystery. **Wanda's Mound** in Nowa Huta is of roughly the same age and size, and is also rumoured to be a burial site, of the legendary Queen Wanda.

Kósciusko's Mound in Zwierzyniec, built in the 1820s, and **Piłsudski's Mound** in Las Wolski, built in the 1930s, honour two military heroes.

at this museum, including some rare British and German aircraft from WWI and Polish planes from WWII. There are over 150 planes in total.

☎ 012 642 87 00 ☐ www.muz-lotnictwa.krakow.pl
✉ Aleja Jana Pawła II 39
€ 7/4zł
🕙 9am-5pm Tue-Fri, 10am-3pm Sat, 10am-4pm Sun May-Oct, 9am-3pm Mon-Fri Nov-Apr
🚌 4, 5, 9, 15, 40
♿ excellent (all ground level)

Silesian House (3, B3)
This former Gestapo HQ today serves as a memorial to those who were tortured and imprisoned here. You can visit the cells, where the prisoners' graffiti can still be seen, and an exhibition on the Polish resistance.

☎ 012 633 14 14
✉ Pomorska 2, Nowa Wieś
€ free
🕙 9am-4pm Tue, Thu-Sat & 2nd Sun of month, 10am-5pm Wed
🚌 4, 8, 13, 14

Wyspiański Museum (4, B3)
Dedicated to the local painter, poet and designer Stanisław Wyspiański (1869–1907), this museum showcases his varied creations, including his stained glass. Also here is his proposed scale model of Wawel Hill, transformed into a cultural Acropolis.

☎ 012 422 70 21
✉ Plac Szczepański 9
€ 7/5zł
🕙 9am-3.30pm Tue-Thu & Sat, 9am-6pm Fri, 10am-3.30pm Sat & Sun

Kraków's first baroque building, the Church of SS Peter & Paul

CHURCHES & SYNAGOGUES

Basilica of the Holy Trinity (4, C5)
Built in 1250 this church was almost destroyed by fire in 1850. The preserved 17th-century cloisters of the adjacent monastery are lined with elaborate tombstones.
✉ Stolarska 12 🚌 1, 6, 7, 8, 18 ♿ fair

Church of Our Lady Queen of Poland (3, off F3)
Commonly known as the Arka Pana (Lord's Ark) this gigantic, concrete boat-shaped church was completed in 1977, after much delay caused by the grudging communist authorities. A 70m-high mast towers above.
✉ Obrońców Krzyża, Nowa Huta 🚌 4, 15 ♿ good

Church of St Andrew (4, C6)
Dating from the late 11th century, this Romanesque church is among the city's oldest structures, and was where local townsfolk sheltered during the Tatar raids of the 13th century. The interior, though, is baroque, featuring lots of gilt, black marble and stucco *putti*.
✉ Grodzka 56

Church of SS Peter & Paul (4, C6)
You can't miss the row of life-sized statues of the Twelve Apostles outside this former Jesuit church, completed in 1622; the dome is Kraków's highest. There are several ornate chapels inside.
✉ Grodzka 52 € transept & crypt 2.50/1zł 🕙 9am-5pm Mon-Sat, 1-5pm Sun

Cistercian Monastery (3, off F3)
The Cistercian Monastery was founded in 1222, and the attached Church of the Holy Virgin and St Wenceslas is famous for its 14th-century

'miraculous crucifix', the sole survivor of a devastating 1447 fire. There's a large park behind.

✉ Klasztorna 11, Mogiła, Nowa Huta 🚊 4, 15 to Plac Centralny, then 20 to Klasztorna ♿ good

Franciscan Church (4, B5)

Founded in the 13th century but largely rebuilt after an 1850 fire, the Franciscan Church is adorned with beautiful stained-glass windows and floral art nouveau murals by Stanisław Wyspiański (p50).

✉ Franciszkańska 🚊 1, 6, 7, 8, 18 ♿ fair

Isaac's Synagogue (6, C2)

In this 17th-century synagogue you can see the remnants of the original murals and watch two word-less historic documentary films, *The Jewish District in 1936* and *The Removal to the Kraków Ghetto* from 1941.

☎ 012 430 55 77 ✉ Kupa 18, Kazimierz € 7/6zł ⏰ 9am-7pm Sun-Fri 🚊 3, 9, 11, 13, 24 ♿ good (all ground level)

Old Synagogue (6, C2)

Built in the 15th century, this is Poland's oldest extant synagogue, though today it's a museum. Exhibitions explain Jewish traditions and culture, and the horrors of the Nazi occupation.

☎ 012 422 09 62 💻 www.mhk.pl ✉ Szeroka 24, Kazimierz € 7/5zł, free Mon ⏰ 10am-2pm Mon, 9am-4pm Wed, Thu, Sat & Sun, 10am-5pm Fri 🚊 3, 9, 11, 13 24 ♿ fair (ground floor)

The soaring spires of the Church of St Andrew (p18)

Remuh Synagogue & Cemetery (6, C2)

Built in the 16th century, this tiny synagogue is the only active Orthodox temple in Kraków. The adjoining cemetery holds more than 700 elaborate, and rare, Renaissance tombstones.

☎ 012 422 12 74 ✉ Szeroka 40, Kazimierz € 5/2zł ⏰ 9am-4pm Mon-Fri 🚊 3, 9, 11, 13, 24 ♿ fair

Tempel Synagogue (6, B2)

Built in the 1860s in the Gothic Revival style, the Tempel Synagogue serves

Kraków's small Reform Jewish community. It has been lovingly restored, and is notable for its beautiful stained-glass windows and polychrome woodwork.

✉ Miodowa 24 € 5/2zł ⏰ 10am-6pm Sun-Fri 🚊 6, 8, 10, 19, 22 ♿ fair

BUILDINGS & MONUMENTS

Barbican (4, D1)

This stocky, turreted brick bastion, with its 3m-thick walls and 130 arrow slits, defended medieval Kraków's northern boundary. It's one of very few such structures that still survive anywhere in Europe.

☎ 012 619 23 20 ✉ Basztowa € 5/3.50zł ⏰ 10.30am-6pm May-Oct 🚊 2, 3, 4, 5, 13

Grunwald Monument (4, D1)

This dramatic monument celebrates the 1410 Battle of Grunwald, when the Poles defeated the Teutonic Knights. The original, erected in 1910, was demolished

NOWA HUTA

The post-war communist authorities in Poland were suspicious of Kraków's 'bourgeois' intellectual and Catholic traditions, and decided that what the city needed was some healthy proletarian influence. So, the Nowa Huta steelworks were constructed 10km east of the historic city centre, along with a planned socialist town to house the workers. Practicality was not an issue – all raw materials, such as coal and iron ore, had to be imported from elsewhere – and the plant, still operating today, has never been profitable. Instead, it has been an environmental disaster, while frequent strikes hastened the demise of the communist regime.

by the Nazis, and this reproduction of it went up in 1975.

✉ Plac Matejki, Kleparz ☉ 24hr 🚌 105, 115, 129, 501 ♿ excellent

Schindler Factory (3, E5)

The industrialist Oskar Schindler saved the lives of many Jews by employing them at this factory during WWII. The building was not open to the public at the time of writing, though a museum is planned for the future.

✉ Lipowa 4, Podgórze 🚊 3, 9, 11, 13, 24

Town Hall Tower (2, A2)

The only surviving section of the medieval town hall, this freestanding tower displays historic photographs. There are panoramic views of the square from the top floor. Note that the steps here are steep and slippery.

☎ 012 619 23 20 ✉ Rynek Główny € 5/3.50zł ☉ 10.30am-2pm & 2.30-6pm Apr-Nov

PARKS & GARDENS

Błonia (3, A-B4)

Błonia is a vast wedge of open meadow where locals walk their dogs, fly kites and go for a jog. Concerts, circuses and other such gatherings take place here.

✉ entry on Aleja Focha & Aleja 3 Maja, Zwierzyniec € free ☉ 24hr 🚌 134, 152, 192 ♿ excellent

Las Wolski (3, off A4)

This huge woodland park, 6km west of the city centre, is a beautiful place for forest walks, and there are

a number of marked trails. In the centre is the **zoo** (see below), while **Piłsudski's Mound** (p17) watches over the north.

✉ Księia Józefa, Tyniec € free ☉ 24hr 🚌 109, 134, 209, 229

Park Jordana (3, B3-4)

This well-maintained park is a lovely spot for an early evening stroll. One end is landscaped with formal flower beds and numerous busts of local worthies, while at the other there are slides, swings and climbing frames for kids.

✉ Aleja 3 Maja € free ☉ 6am-10pm Apr-Oct, 6am-8pm Nov-Mar 🚊 15, 18 ♿ excellent

Planty (4)

This narrow strip of greenery, laid out with numerous statues and benches, encircles the Old Town. It follows the foundations of the city's old defensive walls,

which were demolished in the 19th century.

€ free ☉ 24hr ♿ excellent

KRAKÓW FOR CHILDREN

Kraków Zoo (3, off A4)

Enjoying a wonderful setting in the heart of Las Wolski (see above), Kraków's zoo is home to, among others, chimpanzees, snow leopards, lions, bison and a solitary elephant. Some of the cages are small, but animals look well cared for.

☎ 012 425 35 51 ✉ Las Wolski € 12/6zł ☉ 9am-5pm May-Oct, 9am-3pm Nov-Apr 🚌 134 Ⓟ ♿ excellent

Museum of Municipal Engineering (6, C3)

Tramcars and trucks fill the courtyard of this former depot while inside there's a small collection of cars and motorbikes. A roomful

State-of-the-art splashy fun at Park Wodny (p21)

of hands-on magnetic and water experiments is sure to keep kids occupied too.

☎ 012 421 12 42
🖥 www.mimk.com.pl
✉ Św Wawrzyńca 15, Kazimierz
€ 5.50/3.50zł ☉ 10am-4pm Tue-Sun 🚋 3, 6, 9, 13, 24 ♿ good (all ground level)

Park Wodny (3, F1)

This gigantic water park has three pools, plus several chutes, slides, Jacuzzis and saunas and a climbing wall. In addition, there's a gym, dance studio, beauty salon and restaurant.

☎ 012 616 31 02
🖥 www.parkwodny. pl ✉ Dobrego Pasterza 126 € 1hr-ticket 15/12zł Mon-Fri, 16/14zł Sat & Sun, all-day ticket 33/29zł Mon-Fri, 39/33zł Sat & Sun ☉ 8am-10pm 🚌 125, 129, 139, 152

QUIRKY KRAKÓW

Celestat (3, D3)

This unique museum celebrates the local 'Marksmen's Confraternity',

The Museum of Insurance: slightly more fun than it sounds

a centuries-old shooting club. Rifles, trophies and associated paraphernalia are on show.

☎ 012 429 37 91 🖥 www. mhk.pl ✉ Lubicz 16
€ 5/3.50zł ☉ 9.30am-5pm Tue-Sat May-Oct, 9am-4pm Tue-Sat Nov-Apr
🚋 2, 4, 5, 10, 14, 15 ♿ good

MASTER TWARDOWSKI

Alchemy and magic were popular pastimes in Renaissance Kraków, and the city's leading practitioner of the black arts was a certain Master Piotr Twardowski. Twardowski, legend says, made a Faustian pact with the Devil, receiving unlimited powers in return for his soul. The sorcerer used his powers for good, though, and when one day demons snatched him away, he prayed to the Virgin Mary to be saved. His prayer was answered but, as punishment, he was stranded on the moon, accompanied only by a spider who sometimes dangles down to Kraków to pick up the latest news for the lonely mage.

House under the Spider (3, C3)

Built in 1889, this grand town house is abundantly decorated with Gothic gargoyles. At the top is a big spider sitting at the centre of a web, a nod to local sorcerer Master Twardowski (see box, below left).

✉ Karmelicka 35, Piasek
🚋 4, 8, 13, 14, 24

Museum of Insurance (4, B2)

Documents, insurance policies and 'documents relating to insurance policies' are on display at this small specialist museum, the only one of its kind in Poland. Various advertising materials and portraits complete the collection.

☎ 012 422 88 11
✉ Dunajewskiego 3
€ free ☉ 9-11am Tue-Fri
🚋 2, 7, 8, 15

Trips & Tours

WALKING TOUR
Barbican to Wawel Hill

Set off from the **Barbican** (**1**; p19), heading southwards through the imposing **Florian Gate** (**2**) and down Floriańska. Emerging on the city's main market square, **Rynek Główny** (**3**; p10), you'll see **St Mary's Church** (**4**; p11), with its soaring, uneven towers. Head west across the square, passing through the **Cloth Hall** (**5**; p10), perhaps pausing to view the gallery of paintings upstairs. Continue west along Św Anny, then south on to Jagiellońska, passing the medieval **Collegium Maius** (**6**; p15). Walk south to Gołębia, then turn west on this street to the Planty, to see the neo-Gothic **Collegium Novum** (**7**), the university's main building. Walk southwards through the Planty then head east on Poselska, passing the **Archaeological Museum** (**8**; p16) on the way, until you reach Grodzka. Walk south as far as the **Church of SS Peter and Paul** (**9**; p18) then west on to Kanonicza. Continue south along this cobbled lane, perhaps treating yourself to lunch at **Copernicus** (**10**; p33). At

Distance 1.5km Duration
▶ Start Barbican 🚊 2, 3, 4, 14
● End Wawell Hill 🚌 103, 502

the end of this street, cross Podzamcze and ascend mighty **Wawel Hill** (**11**; p8), topped with the famed Wawel Castle and cathedral.

The magnificent courtyard at Wawel Castle (p8)

DAY TRIPS
Auschwitz-Birkenau (1, A3)

Few words in any language evoke as much horror as Auschwitz. In 1940, on the outskirts of the small town of Oświęcim, the Nazis established a concentration camp which was to become the largest experiment in genocide in the history of humankind. Auschwitz originally held Polish political prisoners, but the camp was then designated as a centre for the extermination of Jews. The main camp was considered too small, so a much larger camp, known as Birkenau or Auschwitz II, was constructed 2km to the west. It has been estimated that around 1.5 million people, including 1.1 million Jews, were systematically murdered here.

Today both camps have been preserved as the Auschwitz-Birkenau State Museum. The smaller Auschwitz camp was only partially destroyed by the fleeing Nazis, and many of the buildings remain. A 15-minute documentary film (2.50zł) in the visitor centre shows the 1945 liberation of the camp, which you enter through the infamous gates bearing the slogan 'Arbeit Macht Frei' (Work Sets You Free). Exhibitions in the barracks are dedicated to the people of various nationalities that died here, while the sight of stacks of human hair – sold to make cloth – is truly shocking. Most mass killings took place at the vast Birkenau camp, and though largely destroyed, the sheer size of the site gives you some idea of the scale of the Nazis' crime.

INFORMATION
60km west of Kraków

- 🚌 bus from Cystersów bus station (9zł, 1½ hr)
- 🅿
- ☎ 033 843 20 22
- 🖥 www.auschwitz-muzeum-oswiecim.pl
- ✉ Więźniów Oświęcimia 20, Oświęcim
- € free; guided tour of Auschwitz 26zł, guided tour of Birkenau 42zł
- ☉ 8am-6pm May & Sep, 8am-7pm Jun-Aug, 8am-5pm Apr & Oct, 8am-4pm Mar & Nov-mid Dec, 8am-3pm mid Dec-Feb
- ⓘ shuttle bus between camps 2zł
- ✗ on-site café

Wieliczka Salt Mine (1, B3)

The Wieliczka Salt Mine no longer produces salt, but guided tours of the old workings take place several times a day in English and less frequently in other languages. The mine, which was in operation for around 700 years, goes down to a depth of 327m, and has been on UNESCO's World Heritage list since 1978.

Tours start with a giddying descent down 380 wooden stairs that reach a depth of some 135m below ground. Thankfully, a lift will whisk you to the top again at the end. Mind your head as you shuffle along; only your guide gets to wear a hard hat. You are taken through a series of chambers, hewn out of the grey-green salt, many with carvings and statues made entirely out of salt by miners. They even carved out chapels for themselves, including the Chapel of St Anthony, from 1689, and the awesome **Chapel of the Blessed Kinga**, measuring 54m by 17m. It took 30 years to create, and was completed in 1927, although various additions, such as a statue of Pope John Paul II, have been made since. Occasional religious services, including weddings, and concerts are held here. Moving on, there are a couple of underground lakes, the inevitable souvenir stalls and a basic restaurant. At the end of the tour is a museum with a display of mining artefacts and more salt sculptures.

INFORMATION

15km southeast of Kraków

- 🚌 minibus from Starowiślna (4, D5; 2.50zł, 20 min)
- 🅿
- ☎ 012 278 73 02
- 🖥 www.kopalina.pl
- ✉ Daniłowicza 10, Wieliczka
- € 2hr guided tours adult/child 55/45zł
- 🕑 7.30am-7.30pm Apr-Oct, 8am-5pm Nov-Mar
- ⓘ Advance ticket sales office in Kraków at Wiślna 12a (4, B4)
- ✖ on-site cafés

Salt statues in an eerie world of pits and chambers

ORGANISED TOURS

Bike Tours in Cracow

See Kraków from a saddle on this four-hour pedal around Wawel Hill, Kazimierz and Stare Miasto, in the company of an English-speaking guide. Tours in other languages can be arranged.

☎ 012 261 07 40
🖥 www.mojerowery.pl
✉ meeting point outside Hotel Royal, Św Gertrudy 26-29
€ 70/35zł ⏱ 9.45am daily

City Tour

Hop on one of these electric golf-buggies for a jaunt around the Old Town or a longer trip to Kazimierz. Multilingual audioguides cost extra.

☎ 012 422 93 04 🖥 www.omega.civ.pl/citytour
✉ buggies leave from Rynek Główny € 1hr 80zł, 2hr 150zł, audioguide 25zł ⏱ vary

Compass

Organises full-day SUV trips to Ojców National Park and the remarkable Błędowska Desert, for a bit of quad-biking. Lunch, dinner and all entrance fees are included. Returns to Kraków about 10pm.

☎ 0500 130 764
🖥 www.expedition.compass.net.pl ✉ arranged meeting point € 575zł ⏱ 8am Mon, Wed & Fri or on request

Cool Tour Company

Runs three guided walks, covering the Old Town, Jewish district and Nowa Huta. Coffee is included,

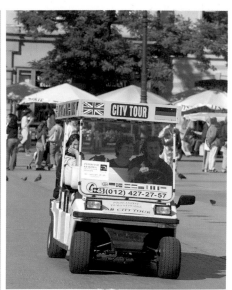
Take the weight off your feet with a buggy tour of the city

along with 'comments and anecdotes' from the guides.

☎ 0509 031 898 🖥 www.cooltourcompany.com
✉ meeting point at the cross at the southern tip of Grodzka € 3hr walk 48zł, 4hr walk 80zł ⏱ Nowa Huta and Kazimierz walks Fri-Sun 10am, city walk Fri-Sun 2pm

Cracow Tours (2, B1)

Offers several bus tours around Kraków and beyond to places like the Wieliczka Salt Mine, Zakopane and even Warsaw (by train). Buses pick up at several hotels.

☎ 012 430 07 26
🖥 www.cracowtours.pl
✉ ticket office in Orbis Travel, Rynek Główny 41
€ city tour 110/55zł, day excursions 255-430zł ⏱ vary, Mar-Nov

Crazy Guides

If you've had enough of bourgeois Kraków, why not explore the workers' paradise of Nowa Huta in a vintage Trabant? Longer trips include an 'interactive Iron Curtain experience', apparently.

☎ 0888 68 68 71 🖥 www.crazyguides.com € 2¹/₂hr tour 119zł, 4hr tour 159zł ⏱ by appointment

Jarden Tourist Agency (6, C1)

Jarden operates tours around sites of Jewish interest, including guided walks of Kazimierz and Podgórze. Tours by car to Auschwitz and places further afield are also possible.

☎ 012 429 13 74 🖥 www.jarden.pl ✉ Szeroka 2, Kazimierz € 2/3hr walking tours 35/45zł, 2hr car tour 65zł ⏱ by appointment

Shopping

Floriańska, Grodzka and Rynek Główny have the greatest concentration of shops in Stare Miasto. Amber jewellery, flavoured vodkas and paintings by local artists are some of the most popular buys. Note that anything made before 1945 is classified as an antique, and you will need an export permit; most shops will arrange this for you. Most big shopping malls are a long way out of town, although the **Nowe Miasto** development, beside the main train station, is scheduled for completion in late 2006.

DEPARTMENT STORES & SHOPPING CENTRES

Galeria Centrum (4, B4)
Men's and women's fashions fill the upper floors of this central department store, while downstairs you'll find a perfumery and cosmetics section. A range of oddments such as scented candles are here too, and women's shoes lurk in the basement.
☎ 012 422 98 22
✉ Św Anny 2 (entry on Wiślna) ☼ 9am-8pm Mon-Fri, 9am-4pm Sat

Galeria Kazimierz (3, D5)
Giant shopping centre on the edge of Kazimierz, housing some 130 outlets for international fashion chains, as well as a large supermarket and a 10-screen cinema (p42). There's also a food court and several coffee bars.
☎ 012 433 01 01 💻 www. galeriakazimierz.pl

✉ Podgórska 34, Kazimierz ☼ 10am-10pm Mon-Sat, 10am-8pm Sun 🚊 3, 9, 11, 13, 24 🅿

Jubilat (3, C4)
It's the handy 24-hour supermarket on the ground floor of this huge eyesore that's the main attraction. Upstairs, departments sell a drab range of clothing plus electronics, carpets, jewellery and other things. There's also a photo-developing lab.
☎ 012 422 80 40 💻 www. jubilat.com.pl ✉ Al Krasińskiego 1, Nowy Świat ☼ supermarket 24hr, other departments 9am-8pm Mon-Fri, 9am-4pm Sat 🚊 1, 2, 6

ARTS & CRAFTS

Alhena (2, C2)
Alhena is an outlet for the high-quality glass products of Poland's famous Krosno factory. Wine glasses, champagne flutes and other practical pieces are here, plus an assemblage of multicoloured vases that might appeal to Granny.
☎ 012 421 54 96 💻 www. alhena.com.pl ✉ Plac Mariacki 1 ☼ 10am-7pm Mon-Fri, 11am-3pm Sat

Cloth Hall (2, B2)
Continually thronged with tourists, the ancient Cloth Hall is lined with numerous stalls selling everything from amber jewellery and wooden chess sets to slippers and T-shirts. It's a handy one-stop shop for grabbing those last-minute souvenirs.
✉ Rynek Główny 1 ☼ 9am-8pm

Gala (6, A1)
Set in the side of the Royal Hotel, Gala stocks an attractive range of traditional Polish ceramics, from colourful stoneware cups, bowls and teapots to some purely decorative pieces. Glassware is also on show.
☎ 012 421 33 66 ✉ Św Gertrudy 26 ☼ 10am-6pm Mon-Fri, 10am-4pm Sat 🚊 6, 8, 10, 18

Galeria Osobliwosci (4, C2)
Step into this fascinating treasure house and you'll probably end up staying longer than you'd imagined. There are cabinets full of fossils, minerals, jewellery, seashells and all manner

Brightly painted wooden crafts in the Cloth Hall

of collectables, as well as paintings and furniture.
☎ 012 429 19 84
✉ Sławkowska 16
🕑 11am-7pm Mon-Fri, 11am-3pm Sat

Galerie d'Art Naïf (6, C2)
Folk art gets a rare showing in this gallery, with a display of 'naïve' paintings and sculptures by local artists. Many of the wooden and ceramic sculptures follow a religious theme, echoing the traditional rural craftsmanship of the past.
☎ 012 421 06 37 🖥 www.artnaive.sky.pl ✉ Józefa 11, Kazimierz 🕑 11am-6pm Mon-Fri, 11am-3pm Sat
🚋 6, 8, 10

Space Gallery (4, D2)
Paintings, drawings and sculptures by contemporary Polish artists, including graduates of Kraków's Academy of Fine Arts, are on sale at this absorbing gallery, along with many 19th- and 20th-century works.
☎ 012 421 89 94 🖥 www.spacegallery.com.pl
✉ 1st floor, Floriańska 13 🕑 10am-6pm Mon-Fri, 10am-3pm Sat

BOOKS & MUSIC

Empik Megastore (2, B2)
It sometimes seems that the entire population of Kraków is being funnelled through this overcrowded shop. International newspapers are on the ground floor, guidebooks, maps, English-, French- and German-language novels are upstairs, while the basement holds a selection of pop, jazz and classical CDs.

Join the throng in the Empik Megastore

☎ 012 429 67 23 🖥 www.empik.com ✉ Rynek Główny 5 🕑 9am-10pm

Jarden Jewish Bookshop (6, C1)
This small bookshop is dedicated to Kraków's Jewish heritage, with numerous titles on Jewish history, culture, cuisine, legends and more, in English and other languages. They also sell guidebooks to Kazimierz (p12), and run tours of sites of Jewish interest (p25).
☎ 012 421 71 66 🖥 www.jarden.pl ✉ Szeroka 2, Kazimierz 🕑 9am-6pm Mon-Fri, 10am-6pm Sat & Sun 🚋 3, 9, 11, 13, 24

Księgarnia Hetmańska (2, B3)
There's a good range of guidebooks and general interest books about Kraków in this venerable bookshop on the main square. English-language novels, including some by Polish authors in translation, are also available.
☎ 012 430 24 53
✉ Rynek Główny 17
🕑 9am-9pm Mon-Sat, 11am-9pm Sun

Kurant (2, B1)
There's a decent range of classical, jazz, Jewish and Polish folk music recordings on sale at Kurant. The shop also specialises in sheet music and song books, and it has a small selection of DVDs.
☎ 012 422 98 59 ✉ Rynek Główny 36 🕑 9am-7pm Mon-Fri, 10am-3pm Sat

Massolit Books (3, C4)
Massolit is an English-language bookshop selling new and second-hand titles covering history, philosophy, Jewish studies, literary criticism and other academic subjects, as well as countless novels. There's a small café on site too.
☎ 012 432 41 50 🖥 www.massolit.com ✉ Felicjanek 4, Nowy Świat 🕑 10am-8pm Sun-Thu, 10am-10pm Fri & Sat 🚋 1, 2, 6

Music Corner (2, B3)
On the second floor of Pasaż Handlowy Rynek 13, Music Corner has a varied assortment of CDs. Browse through classical, jazz, pop, rock, heavy metal and folk

recordings or flip through their second-hand vinyl.
☎ 012 617 02 02
💻 www.musiccorner.pl
✉ Rynek Główny 13
🕒 10am-8pm Mon-Fri, 10am-7pm Sat & Sun

FOR CHILDREN

Bajo (6, A1)
Bajo focuses on good old-fashioned playthings, mostly made out of wood. Giant doll's houses, rocking horses, trains, puzzles and plenty of other quality handmade toys offer a welcome alternative to the more usual mass-produced plastic.
☎ 012 292 06 44 💻 www.bajotoys.com ✉ Grodzka 60
🕒 10am-6pm Mon-Fri, 10am-2pm Sat

Galeria Bukowski (2, C3)
Countless teddy bears, from pocket-sized to near life-size, pack this place from floor to ceiling. There are many different kinds, all with their own names, and a veritable menagerie of cuddly ducks, rabbits and cats adds a touch of variety.

☎ 012 433 88 55 💻 www.galeriabukowski.pl
✉ Sienna 1 🕒 10am-7pm Mon-Fri, 10am-6pm Sat

Smyk (3, D5)
This chain store outlet inside the Galeria Kazimierz shopping centre (p26) is packed with soft toys, board games, action figures and more, mostly aimed at younger children. It also sports a collection of clothes and shoes.
☎ 012 433 01 28 ✉ 1st floor Galeria Kazimierz
🕒 10am-8pm 🚊 3, 9, 11, 13, 24 🅿

JEWELLERY & CLOTHING

The Amber Chamber (4, D2)
Enter the Amber Chamber for all your honey coloured fossilised tree resin requirements. There's a big selection of amber jewellery on offer, including some impractically chunky looking necklaces, as well as more tasteful rings and earrings.

☎ 012 431 07 50 💻 www.amber.com.pl ✉ Floriańska 42 🕒 10am-9pm Mon-Sat, 10am-8pm Sun 🚊 3, 4, 5, 13, 15

Błażko Kindery (6, C2)
The eye-catching creations of Grzegorz Błażko are on display in this little shop, including his unique range of chequered enamel rings, pendants, bracelets, earrings and cufflinks. Most are silver.
☎ 012 430 67 31 💻 www.blazko.pl ✉ Józefa 11, Kazimierz 🕒 11am-7pm Mon-Fri, 11am-3pm Sat 🚊 6, 8, 10

Galeria Skarbiec (4, C5)
Colourful and contemporary jewellery fills the window of this attractive store, with necklaces, brooches, rings and earrings made with semi-precious stones. Amber is also much in evidence.
☎ 012 422 60 56
✉ Grodzka 35 🕒 10am-7pm Mon-Fri, 10am-3pm Sat

Punkt (3, C4)
Colourful women's clothes and accessories, including a

CLOTHING & SHOE SIZES

Women's Clothing

Aust/UK	8	10	12	14	16	18
Europe	36	38	40	42	44	46
Japan	5	7	9	11	13	15
USA	6	8	10	12	14	16

Women's Shoes

Aust/USA	5	6	7	8	9	10
Europe	35	36	37	38	39	40
France only	35	36	38	39	40	42
Japan	22	23	24	25	26	27
UK	3½	4½	5½	6½	7½	8½

Men's Clothing

Aust	92	96	100	104	108	112
Europe	46	48	50	52	54	56

Japan	S	M	M		L	
UK/USA	35	36	37	38	39	40

Men's Shirts (Collar Sizes)

Aust/Japan	38	39	40	41	42	43
Europe	38	39	40	41	42	43
UK/USA	15	15½	16	16½	17	17½

Men's Shoes

Aust/UK	7	8	9	10	11	12
Europe	41	42	43	44½	46	47
Japan	26	27	27.5	28	29	30
USA	7½	8½	9½	10½	11½	12½

Measurements approximate only; try before you buy.

AMBER

Look in any jewellery shop window in Kraków and you'll see a host of golden globules of fossilised tree resin. Although found all over the world, the largest deposits of amber are washed up along the Baltic coast. This precious organic substance was formed 40–60 million years ago, when the region was covered with dense subtropical forests, and it has been traded for at least 12,000 years. Today you can buy everything from a nifty pair of cufflinks to a Flintstones-style chunky necklace.

selection of handbags and jewellery, are on sale at this fashionable boutique. Some of the pieces are one-offs created by local designer Monika.
☎ 0502 600 410
🖳 www.punkt.sklep.pl
✉ Podzamcze 22
🕙 1-8pm 🚌 103, 502

FOOD & DRINK

Likus Concept Store (2, B3)

In the basement of the Pasaż Handlowy Rynek 13 shopping centre, this 'concept store' is divided into a well stocked upmarket delicatessen, a fine wine shop and a café. There's also a small china and glassware shop.
☎ 012 617 02 27 ✉ Rynek Główny 13 🕙 11am-9pm Mon-Sat, 11am-5pm Sun

Szambelan (2, A3)

The big-bellied urns of colourful liquids lining the shelves at Szambelan may call to mind an old apothecary, but it's vodka that's being prescribed here. Sample varieties flavoured with raspberry, coffee, mountain ash or honey; then buy an empty bottle of whatever size you want, and have it filled.
☎ 012 430 24 09
🖳 www.szambelan.com.pl ✉ Gołębia 2 (entry on Bracka) 🕙 10am-8pm Mon-Sat, noon-5pm Sun

Toruńskie Pierniki (2, B3)

This sweet-smelling little shop sells a selection of delectable gingerbread and other sweets, produced in Toruń. The traditional treat comes in a variety of forms, including hard baked figurines and little cakes filled with marmalade.
☎ 012 431 13 06
✉ Grodzka 14 🕙 11am-7pm Mon-Fri, 10am-6pm Sat & Sun

Wawel (2, A2)

This charmingly old-world little chocolate shop sells the products of Kraków's home grown confectionery company. Choose from an assortment of loose chocolates, or try one of the numerous bars and fancier boxes of chocolates.
☎ 012 423 12 47
✉ Rynek Główny 33
🕙 9am-6pm

MARKET DAY

Kraków has a few open-air markets where you can purchase all the fresh fruit, vegetables and bread you could want, as well as a variety of cheap clothes, which you probably won't want. Most convenient for the Old Town is the **Stary Kleparz Market** (4, D1; Rynek Kleparski, Kleparz), while further north is **Nowy Kleparz Market** (3, C3; Plac Nowy Kleparz). Both are open roughly 6am-6pm Monday-Saturday.

Plac Nowy (6, B2) in Kazimierz also hosts a daily fruit and vegetable market, while on Sundays it fills up with new and second-hand clothes stalls. It's usually over by 3pm.

Eating

The sheer range and quality of restaurants in Kraków might surprise you. Dumplings certainly still feature on many a menu, but here, besides sampling top-class contemporary Polish cuisine, you can also dine at restaurants specialising in French, Indian, Hungarian, Japanese and Brazilian food, to name just a few, while Italian cuisine seems to be very much in favour all across town. Most restaurants are to be found in the Old Town (Stare Miasto) and in Kazimierz, which has some outstanding eateries well worth seeking out.

MEAL COSTS

The prices in this chapter indicate the cost of a two-course meal with one drink for one person.

€	up to 25zł
€€	25–45zł
€€€	46–70zł
€€€€	over 70zł

AROUND RYNEK GŁÓWNY

Grill 15/16 (2, B3)
Steakhouse €€€
The summer courtyard garden at this busy restaurant provides an attractive atmosphere for enjoying the grilled meat, steaks and fish served here. Dishes include 'fresh trout roasted over volcanic lava rocks', venison, T-bone steaks and salads, and there's a short children's menu too.
☎ 012 424 96 00 🖳 www.grill15-16.pl ✉ Rynek Główny 16 🕑 noon-midnight 🚼 Ⓥ

Pizza Club Oskar (2, B3)
Pizzeria €
Oskar is basically a nightclub with a bar serving food of the pizza and pasta persuasion, though it's tasty and reasonably priced. You can take in a game of darts or pool in adjoining rooms afterwards, while the disco gets going on Friday and Saturday nights. There's outdoor seating if you prefer.
☎ 012 421 06 83 ✉ 1st floor, Rynek Główny 9 🕑 11am-midnight Ⓥ

Sioux (2, A2)
Tex-Mex, Steakhouse €€
Kids will love this bustling Wild West-themed chain restaurant, draped with wagon wheels, harnesses and other ranch paraphernalia. Waiters dressed as cowboys will bring you your choice of burritos, fajitas, steaks, ribs and the like. Yee-ha!
☎ 012 421 34 62 🖳 www.sioux.krakow.pl ✉ Rynek Główny 22 🕑 11am-midnight 🚼 Ⓥ

Szara (2, B2)
International €€€€
This upmarket restaurant on the main square offers a wide-ranging menu of international and fusion cuisine in stately surrounds. Bouillabaisse, lamb chops, chicken stuffed with smoked salmon, and salmon in teriyaki sauce are just a few of the tempting dishes.
☎ 012 421 66 69 🖳 www.szara.pl ✉ Rynek Główny 6 🕑 11am-11pm

Café society on Rynek Główny

Wierzynek (2, B3)
Polish €€€€
A Kraków landmark, Wierzynek is a grand, antique-stuffed place that has played host to various visiting dignitaries over the years, including Fidel Castro. The cuisine is a combination of classic Polish and French, and includes venison, pike and duck.
☎ 012 424 96 00 🖳 www.wierzynek.com.pl
✉ Rynek Główny 15
🕑 1pm-midnight

NORTHERN STARE MIASTO

Bombaj Tandoori (4, D4)
Indian €€
Kraków's best curry house has a big menu of Indian standards, including vegetarian options and decent garlic naans. The 14zł lunch special is good value, and the Indian beers and teas are well worth sampling. The rickety wicker seating needs throwing out though.
☎ 012 422 37 97
✉ Mikołajska 11
🕑 noon-11pm Sun-Thu, noon-midnight Fri & Sat Ⓥ

Cyrano de Bergerac (4, C2)
French €€€€
Furnished with antiques, this award-winning restaurant has earned a high reputation for its take on traditional French cuisine. Caviar, foie gras, chateaubriand and scallops are all on offer, along with such delicacies as sweetbreads fried with walnuts.
☎ 012 411 72 88 🖳 www.cyranodebergerac.pl
✉ Sławkowska 26

Veggie treats draw the crowds at Green Way

🕑 noon-midnight Mon-Sat
🚊 2, 3, 4, 5, 7, 14

Del Papà (4, C2)
Italian €€
Del Papà is a modish little restaurant serving up some great Italian cooking in an intimate setting. The four-course lunch menus, at 29zł and 39zł, are superb value, and there's a big list of pizzas and pasta to try.
☎ 012 421 83 43
🖳 www.delpapa.pl ✉ Św Tomasza 6
🕑 11.30am-11pm ♿ fair ♿ Ⓥ

Farina (4, C2)
Seafood €€€
Being so far inland, Kraków doesn't go in much for seafood, but Farina is a welcome exception. Mussels, oysters, dorado and sea bass are among the high-quality fishy ingredients, and they also offer homemade pasta. There's a separate children's menu too.
☎ 012 422 16 80 🖳 www.farina.krakow.pl

✉ Św Marka 16
🕑 noon-11pm 🚊 2, 4, 7, 13, 14 ♿

Green Way (4, D3)
Vegetarian €
Great-value meat-free fare is available at Green Way, including enchiladas, salads, veggie burgers and various other choices, which change daily. There's also a good variety of drinks. It's a small but very popular place, so you'll probably end up sharing a table.
☎ 012 431 10 27
✉ Mikołajska 14 🕑 10am-10pm Mon-Fri, 11am-9pm Sat & Sun ♿ Ⓥ

Ipanema (4, D3)
Brazilian €€
Coffee grinders and bananas decorate this cheerful Brazilian restaurant, which serves generous platefuls of roast chicken and beef dishes, and the range of unusual 'Afro-Brazilian' dishes includes some seafood combinations. Most meals are accompanied

with a dose of good old Polish cabbage.

☎ 012 422 53 23 🖳 www.ipanema.com.pl ✉ Św Tomasza 28 🕑 noon-11pm Mon-Thu, noon-midnight Fri-Sun **V**

Leonardo (4, D3)
Italian €€€€
Sample some exemplary Italian cuisine at the subterranean Leonardo, a popular spot with both locals and visitors. The usual pasta dishes are all there, as well as some intriguing, and beautifully presented, house specialities such as zander fillet in caramel sauce.

☎ 012 429 68 50
🖳 www.leonardo.com.pl
✉ Szpitalna 20 🕑 11am-11pm 🚃 2, 3, 4, 5, 13 **V**

Metropolitan (4, C3)
International €€€
Attached to the Hotel Saski (p45), Metropolitan is a snazzy, cosmopolitan place filled with photographs of London. It's popular with foreign visitors, who turn up for the especially good breakfasts. Fish, duck, pasta and steak are on the lunch and dinner menus.

☎ 012 421 98 03
✉ Sławkowska 3
🕑 7.30am-midnight Mon-Sat, 7.30am-10pm Sun

Nikita Bar (4, C2)
Café €
Adorned with Russian theatrical posters, this tiny 'coffee and lunch bar' is an appealing spot for a light meal of dumplings, salads, pasta or blinis, with either sweet or savoury toppings. They also serve good breakfasts, cakes and drinks.

✉ Sławkowska 26
🕑 9am-7pm 🚃 2, 4, 13 **V**

Orient Ekspres (4, C4)
International €€€
One of the best restaurants in town, the stylish Orient Ekspres attempts to re-create the atmosphere of the golden age of steam with its retro décor, though the food is entirely contemporary. The butterfish is superb, while other dishes worth trying include steaks and pasta.

☎ 012 422 66 72 🖳 www.orient-ekspres.krakow.pl
✉ Stolarska 13 🕑 noon-11pm 🚃

Pierogarnia (4, C2)
Polish €
If you've developed a taste for *pierogi* (Polish dumplings), or if you're just looking for something quick and cheap, this tiny restaurant serves nine types, including meat, mushroom and fruit-filled varieties. There are only

---

OBWARZANKI & OSCYPKI

No, not a Polish comedy double-act but two cheap local food products you should try before leaving Kraków. *Obwarzanki* are hard, ring-shaped bread rolls similar to bagels, and sold from handcarts across the city. They come with three toppings – sesame seeds, poppy seeds or salt crystals. They cost 1zł, and are particularly popular as a quick breakfast snack.

Oscypki are unpasteurised smoked sheep's cheeses, traditionally made by highland shepherds. You'll see these golden-coloured cheeses, pressed into patterned cylindrical shapes, being sold by old ladies on Floriańska and elsewhere in Kraków, but it may be safer to buy them at supermarkets.

five tables, and locals are willing to queue.

☎ 012 422 74 95
✉ Sławkowska 32
⏲ 10am-9pm 🚃 2, 4, 5, 7, 14, 15, 24 V

Pod Ogródkiem (2, A1)
Café €

This simple place specialises in Breton-style buckwheat *gallettes* (pancakes), with a huge choice of savoury or sweet fillings including sheep's cheese and sausage. They also do a few salads, and it's a quiet place for a beer or two as well. At the front there's a bookshop selling maps.

☎ 012 292 07 63
✉ Jagiellońska 6 ⏲ noon-midnight ♿ good 🍴 V

Polakowski (4, C2)
Polish €

If it's simple, wholesome food you're after, then this cheery self-service restaurant might be the answer. Try soups, dumplings or chicken-and-potatoes type dishes with a glass of cold Tyskie beer. Hardly gourmet offerings, but very tasty nonetheless, and the potato soup is excellent. There's another branch in Kazimierz, at Miodowa 39 (6, C1).

☎ 012 422 48 22 ✉ Św Tomasza 5 ⏲ 10am-10pm 🍴 V

Smaki Świata (4, D2)
Vegetarian €

There's a diverse choice of mostly vegetarian and vegan meals to be had at this friendly restaurant, including Mexican, Greek and Indian options – the 'true Indian thali' snack set is delicious. There's a separate sushi menu,

---

MUNCH SOME DUMPLINGS

Wherever you go in Poland you'll come across the little boiled dumplings called *pierogi*, and Kraków is no exception. In fact, one restaurant, Pierogarnia (p32), serves little else. The most popular varieties are *ruskie* (filled with cottage cheese and potato), *z kapustą i grzybami* (with cabbage and mushrooms), *z serem* (with cheese), *z mięsem* (with meat) and *z owocami* (stuffed with fruit). Usually served without any sauce, other than some butter or oil, or maybe some fried onions, they are hugely popular and very cheap. You're unlikely to pay more than 10zł for a plateful.

---

a few chicken dishes and a big list of teas to choose from.

☎ 012 421 17 21 💻 www. smakiswiata.pl ✉ Szpitalna 38 ⏲ 9am-10pm Mon-Sat, 10am-10pm Sun 🚃 2, 3, 4, 5, 13, 14 V

Szlacheckie Jadło (4, C2)
Polish €€€

Listen out for the flutey medieval music emanating from this armour-bedecked place, or look for the dummy knight guarding the doorway, and prepare for a boisterous banqueting experience. Live music and waiters in fancy dress accompany the traditional Polish game, flaming pork skewers and mixed grills.

☎ 012 422 74 95 💻 www. szlacheckiejadlo.pl ✉ Sławkowska 32 ⏲ 11am-11pm 🚃 2, 4, 7, 13

SOUTHERN STARE MIASTO

Aqua e Vino (4, B4)
Italian €€€

This stone-vaulted cellar provides a sophisticated setting for authentic Italian cuisine, prepared by an authentic Italian chef called

---

Francesco. The pasta is first-rate, as are the grilled meat dishes such as duck breast in Cabernet sauce. It's frequented by Italian tourists, which must be a good sign.

☎ 012 421 25 67 💻 www. aquaevino.pl ✉ Wiślna 5 ⏲ 11.30am-midnight V

Bar Vega (4, D5)
Vegetarian €

Exclusively vegetarian, Bar Vega has an impressively varied menu including such things as soy or oat cutlets, pancakes, dumplings, casseroles and breakfasts, as well as a lengthy list of teas. It's a bright, appealing place and a hit with locals.

☎ 012 422 34 94
💻 www.vegarestauracja. com.pl
✉ Św Gertrudy 7
⏲ 9am-9pm 🚃 6, 8, 10, 18 ♿ V

Copernicus (4, C6)
International €€€€

The restaurant of the top-class hotel of the same name (p44), Copernicus certainly doesn't disappoint. Guinea fowl in grape sauce, duck, salmon, rabbit and

Many places offer hearty Polish fare in homely surroundings

pigeon all appear on the inventive menu, and service is pleasingly attentive.
☎ 012 424 34 21
✉ Kanonicza 16
🕑 noon-11pm
🚋 103, 502

Kawaleria (2, A3)
Polish €€
Kawaleria is an elegant, equine-themed restaurant filled with sepia photographs of old Poland. Contemporary Polish cooking is served, and the 19.50zł lunch specials are a bargain. The mushroom soup with hazelnuts is very good, while roast pork and chicken dishes are among the mainstays.
☎ 012 430 24 32 🖳 www.kawaleria.com ✉ Gołębia 4
🕑 11am-midnight
🚋 1, 6, 7, 8, 18

Kwadrans Lunch Bar (4, C5)
Café €
Set back in a quiet courtyard off busy Grodzka, Kwadrans

offers simple dishes such as dumplings, pasta, salads, soups and chicken cutlets. It's a pleasant place to relax with an alfresco beer or two as well.
☎ 012 294 22 22
✉ Grodzka 32 🕑 9.30am-11pm 🚻 Ⓥ

Pod Temidą (4, C5)
Café €
One of Kraków's few remaining socialist-era milk bars, Pod Temidą looks like an industrial works canteen, and the menu on the wall is only in Polish, but it's all good, sturdy food, and remarkably cheap; expect the usual *pierogi,* soups and *bigos* (meat and cabbage stew).
☎ 012 422 08 74
✉ Grodzka 43 🕑 9am-8pm 🚻 Ⓥ

Różowy Słoń (4, A4)
Café €
The 'Pink Elephant' is one of Kraków's brighter and more inviting self-service milk

bars, with Roy Liechtenstein-style cartoons plastering its walls. It's popular with students, who come here for the cheap grills, soups and dumplings.
☎ 012 421 10 47
✉ Straszewskiego 24
🕑 9am-9pm Mon-Sat, 10am-9pm Sun 🚋 2, 7, 8, 15 🚻 Ⓥ

Smak Ukraiński (4, C6)
Ukrainian €€
Tucked inside a cellar decorated with typical folksy flair, this place serves up traditional Ukrainian food, which involves lots of borscht and dumplings. There's occasional live music, and a ground-level café offering drinks and cakes.
☎ 012 421 92 94 🖳 www.ukrainska.pl ✉ Kanonicza 15 🕑 11am-9pm Ⓥ

Szabla i Szklanka (4, C5)
Hungarian, Polish €€
You can pick and choose from the two separate Hungarian and Polish menus at this colourful restaurant, decked out with bunches of paprika and toy horses. On the Hungarian side, the goose is excellent, while pork, beef and duck figure on the Polish menu. Round it off with a good glass of tokaj. Or vodka.
☎ 012 426 54 40
✉ Poselska 22 🕑 noon-11pm

KAZIMIERZ

Alef (6, C2)
Jewish €€
This self-consciously quaint restaurant, filled with an-tique furnishings, paintings and mirrors, offers Jewish food such as carp, goose and

chicken *knedlach,* along with some Polish standards. It's not exactly kosher, but it's an attractive place to imbibe the atmosphere of old Kazimierz.
☎ 012 421 38 70 ⌨ www.alef.pl ✉ Szeroka 17 ☽ 9am-11pm ☷ 3, 7, 13, 24 ♿ fair

Arka Noego (6, C2)
Jewish €€
'Noah's Ark' provides the typical Kazimierz eating experience, with lacy tablecloths, candles, a scattering of antiques and a vaguely Jewish-inspired menu. Dumplings, fish and turkey are offered, along with a big drinks list, including kosher vodka. There's live music most evenings after 8pm, with an extra charge of 20zł.
☎ 012 429 15 28 ✉ Szeroka 2 ☽ 10am-midnight Mon-Thu, 10am-2am Fri-Sat ☷ 3 ♿ fair

Klezmer Hois (6, C2)
Jewish €€
Located in the hotel of the same name (p45), Klezmer Hois is yet another of the antique-cluttered spaces in Kazimierz serving Jewish cuisine, and is probably the best of the bunch. Enjoy one of the nightly music performances while tucking into Jewish caviar, stuffed goose necks, baked duck or carp.
☎ 012 411 12 45 ⌨ www.klezmer.pl ✉ Szeroka 6 ☽ 9am-10pm ☷ 3, 11, 13 ♿

Kuchnia i Wino (6, C2)
Mediterranean €€€
This cosy little restaurant, complete with blazing log

fire in winter, is one of Kazimierz's best dining spots. Fresh fish is available from Thursday to Sunday, and new dishes are marked up on a blackboard. The salads are excellent too. Otherwise try chicken or beef, with a good glass of wine.
☎ 012 421 77 36 ✉ Józefa 13 ☽ noon-11pm ☷ 6, 8, 10

Once Upon a Time in Kazimierz (6, C1)
Polish €€
Outwardly resembling a row of old Jewish shops and with an interior cluttered with carpentry tools, tailors' dummies and other oddments, this is an evocative place for a candle-lit dinner. The food – dumplings and simple grills – is an anticlimax, though the garlic soup is tasty.
☎ 012 421 21 17 ✉ Szeroka 1 ☽ 10am-midnight ☷ 3, 9, 11, 13, 24 Ⓥ

Pepe Rosso (6, C2)
Italian €€€
Excellent Italian cuisine is the order of the day at Pepe Rosso. Enjoy some good

home-made pasta, risotto, grilled meat or fish in the brick-vaulted cellar, or in lighter surrounds on the ground floor. The tiramisu is very good, and service quick and friendly.
☎ 012 431 08 75 ✉ Kupa 15 ☽ 9am-11pm ☷ 3, 9, 11, 13, 24 Ⓥ

Restauracja Galicja (6, C1)
Polish €€
Traditional Galician and Polish game dishes are the speciality of this welcoming modern restaurant, with venison making multiple appearances on the menu. Pork is another favourite, and there's a big list of soups too. Dine upstairs or in the atmospheric brick-vaulted cellars.
☎ 012 429 26 07 ✉ Starowiślna 71 ☽ 11am-11pm ☷ 3, 9, 11, 13, 24 ♿

Sami Swoi (3, D5)
Pub Grub €€
Right beside the Galeria Kazimierz shopping centre (p26), Sami Swoi offers the regulation dumplings and sausages, as well as lots of 'beer snacks' such as roasted

MILK BARS
Milk bars *(bar mleczny)* were designed as cheap, no-frills caféterias, subsidised by the state during the communist era, in order to provide simple, wholesome meals for the poorest citizens. The 'milk' part of the name reflects the fact that a large part of the menu was based on dairy products. The 'free market' forced many of these places to close, but some in Kraków have survived by introducing meat dishes and varying their menus. Though prices have risen, these are still the cheapest places to eat. Pod Temidą and Różowy Słoń (p34) are prime examples.

Cyrano de Bergerac (p31) serves top-notch French cuisine

plums wrapped in bacon and fried camembert. Upstairs there's a pub with a giant TV screen and comfy sofas, which packs out nightly.
☎ 012 433 01 91
✉ Podgórska 34 ☽ 10am-last customer ⛟ 3, 9, 11, 13, 24 Ⓟ Ⓥ

Villa Kazimierz (6, C2)
International €€€
The varied menu here includes beef sirloin, trout, duck and, interestingly, 'salmon-flavoured chicken in cauliflower cream'. It's a fresh, upscale place with a pleasant summer garden, and offers a contrast to the chintzy restaurants which dominate this area.
☎ 012 422 67 90 ⛘ www.villakazimierz.pl ✉ Szeroka 39 ☽ noon-11pm ⛟ 3, 9, 11, 13, 24 ⛾ fair

WORTH A TRIP

A Dong (3, D5)
Asian €€
For Kraków's best Chinese and Asian food, dine in

A Dong, on the south side of the River Wisła. It's well regarded locally for its seafood and duck, while the Mongolian barbecue, cooked at your table, is an experience in itself.
☎ 012 656 48 72
✉ Brodzińskiego 3, Podgórze ☽ 11am-11pm ⛟ 6, 8, 10

Café Manggha (3, C5)
Japanese €€
Tucked inside the Manggha Centre of Japanese Art & Technology (p17), this airy café claims to serve the best sushi in town, which is no doubt correct given the scant competition here. The food is authentic, though, and there's also a big choice of Japanese teas. From the outdoor terrace you can enjoy great views of Wawel Castle.
☎ 012 267 27 03
✉ Konopnickiej 26, Dębniki ☽ 10am-7pm Tue-Thu, 10am-8pm Fri-Sun ⛟ 103, 124, 144, 164 ⛾ good Ⓥ

Jarema (4, E1)
Polish, Lithuanian €€€
Just north of the Old Town, Jarema is a rather formal place to try some good-quality traditional Polish food. They focus on the cuisines of the old Polish lands in the east, now part of Lithuania and Ukraine, with lots of game and other meat, though vegetarian options are available.
☎ 012 429 36 69 ⛘ www.jarema.pl ✉ Plac Matejki 5 ☽ noon-10pm ⛟ 105, 115, 501 ⛾ Ⓥ

PescaBar (4, A2)
Café €
A short walk west of the Old Town, PescaBar is a bright and cheerful self-service cafeteria with a vaguely marine theme. There are various fish dishes on the menu, along with pasta, tortillas and other cheap eats.
☎ 012 423 25 13
✉ Karmelicka 14, Piasek ☽ 11am-10pm ⛟ 4, 8, 13, 14, 24

Entertainment

There's plenty going on in Kraków at all times of year, with a packed programme of festivals and numerous smaller events, with venues ranging from the grand Filharmonia Krakowska and Słowacki Theatre, with their offerings of classical concerts and opera, to atmospheric cellar-dwelling jazz clubs proffering some late-night sax. There are numerous more contemporary places to let your hair down too, including big, brash dance clubs and countless traditional pubs.

Many Kraków pubs are in atmospheric but smoky cellars

Although it receives nowhere near as many visitors as cities such as Prague, Kraków is gaining in popularity. British stag parties have begun arriving, although numbers are still very small, and most pubs and bars are geared very much towards the locals. This means smoke-filled cellars for the most part, and a curious aversion to lighting, so do watch your step on those uneven stone stairs. There are many smarter, ground-level bars if you'd prefer a bit more oxygen. Most of the clubs in the city centre operate quite a strict door selection policy, so dress smartly, and note that bouncers can take a very 'hands-on' approach with anyone who's had a few too many.

Kraków has a long theatrical tradition, and its playhouses are legendary. Cabaret too, is a vibrant local institution, with provincial political satire and slapstick forming the basis of most acts. Needless to say, you'll need fluent Polish to appreciate these art forms.

There are a few publications with details of what's on around town. *This Month in Kraków* has information in English on concerts, exhibitions and so on, as does *Karnet*, which covers the more cultural events. The free brochure *Krakout* has less detailed listings and comes out twice monthly in summer, monthly at other times.

You will be able to book tickets for all kinds of events at the Cultural Information Centre (p57).

Coffee and fresh air at a Kazimierz café

BARS & PUBS

Boogie (4, D3)

This smart, fashionable bar, bedecked with black and white photos of Duke Ellington and other jazz greats, is a cool place to hang out with a cocktail or two. They also serve light meals including pasta, salads and sandwiches.
☎ 012 429 43 06
✉ Szpitalna 9
🕙 10am-2am

C K Browar (4, A2)

This subterranean microbrewery and beer hall serves its own brews, including wheat and ginger varieties, and you can even have your own private tap brought to your table. It's an airless place, though, and the pounding Bon Jovi soundtrack and dense fug of cigarette smoke won't appeal to everyone.
☎ 012 429 25 05
✉ Podwale 6 🕙 9am-2am
🚋 2, 7, 8, 15

Free Pub & Dekafencja (2, A1)

The ground-level Dekafencja, with its wood-beamed ceiling and darts machine, offers both alcohol and coffee, while the Free Pub in the cellar is a more traditional beer hall; dark, smoky, candles on tables and lots of steps to trip over and fall down.
☎ 012 802 90 82
✉ Sławkowska 4 🕙 11am-last customer

Nic Nowego (4, D4)

'Nothing New' is a bright and welcoming Irish bar, thankfully without the usual tweeness and 'jolly-Irish-pub-song' soundtrack, though they do serve Guinness. Breakfast and light meals can be had too.
☎ 012 421 61 88 🖥 www.nicnowego.com ✉ Św Krzyża 15 🕙 7am-last customer

Oldsmobil (4, D3)

Decorated throughout with pictures of classic cars, Oldsmobil is one of central Kraków's quieter and more old-fashioned bars, with a generally older clientele. It also serves coffee and light meals, though the much advertised cocktails are a bit amateurish.
☎ 012 292 07 43 ✉ Św Tomasza 31 🕙 noon-last customer Mon-Fri, 4pm-last customer Sat & Sun

Shisha Club (4, D4)

In the basement of the Casa della Pizza restaurant, Shisha offers a taste of the kasbah, complete with Middle Eastern music, hookah pipes and belly-dancing in suitably Oriental surroundings. Food is also available.
☎ 012 421 64 98 🖥 www.shisha.pl ✉ Mały Rynek 2 🕙 noon-midnight

Transylwania (6, C2)

For a Gothic night out, try this cramped vampire-themed bar in Kazimierz, complete with open coffin in the corner, pictures of old Vlad, spluttering candles and numerous mirrors to check your fellow drinkers' reflections. There are occasional tarot card readings.
☎ 692 320 946 ✉ Szeroka 9, Kazimierz 🕙 10am-2am
🚋 3, 9, 11, 13, 24

U Kacpra (2, A1)

Just off the main square, the brick-vaulted U Kacpra is your regular Kraków pub; dark, subterranean and heaving in the evening. If you can get a seat, it's an atmospheric place for a round of cold beers.
☎ 012 421 88 26
✉ Sławkowska 2
🕙 noon-2am

Vinoteka La Bodega (4, C2)

This stylish wine bar is a great place to enjoy a glass or two of quality vino while munching some tapas and watching silent football on the giant TV screen. There's

---

VODKA

Poles certainly appreciate their vodka, and there's a surprisingly wide array of both natural and flavoured varieties to choose from. There are even bars and shops in Kraków that specialise in the potent spirit. Natural, clear vodkas include Kraków's very own *Cracovia* and *Chopin,* which is made from potatoes, while perhaps the best-known of Poland's flavoured vodkas is *Żubrówka,* which is infused with 'bison grass' from the Białowieska Forest in the north. Another popular tipple is *krupnik,* a golden, honey-flavoured vodka, while there are literally hundreds of others flavoured with a great variety of aromatic herbs and fruits.

also a well-stocked wine shop at the back.
☎ 012 425 49 81 🖳 www.bodega.pl ✉ Sławkuwska 12 ⌚ 10am-midnight

Wódka (4, D4)
No need for fancy names at this little bar. At 'Vodka' you can choose from dozens of different Polish and foreign vodkas, just to see which one is your *real* favourite…
☎ 012 422 32 14 ✉ Mikołajska 5 ⌚ 10am-2pm Mon-Fri, noon-2am Sat & Sun

CLUBS

Alchemia (6, C2)
Decked out with the usual retro Kazimierz knick-knackery, Alchemia offers one of the best line-ups of live music acts in town, including jazz, blues and pop. There's also a small cinema, and various other events are organised.
☎ 012 421 22 00 🖳 www.alchemia.com.pl ✉ Estery 5, Kazimierz € concerts 30-50zł, cinema 9zł ⌚ 9am-3am 🚋 3, 6, 8, 10

Frantic (2, A1)
With two dance floors, three bars, a chill-out room and top Polish and international DJs, Frantic is regularly packed out with smart young locals. There's sniffy door selection, so don't be too scruffy.
☎ 012 423 04 83 🖳 www.frantic.pl ✉ Szewska 5 € varies ⌚ 6pm-4am Tue-Sun 🚋 2, 4, 7, 8, 14

Fshut (6, C2)
This subterranean Kazimierz club plays everything from reggae to house music every

Party till the wee small hours at Fshut

night, with guest DJs at the weekend. Artsy offerings such as film screenings, exhibitions and fashion shows also take place.
☎ 012 429 26 09 🖳 www.fshut.com ✉ Szeroka 10, Kazimierz € varies ⌚ 5pm-4am 🚋 3, 9, 11, 13, 24

Midgard (4, D2)
No Vikings, sadly, but this subterranean cavern is a huge place, with snazzy sofas to lounge on and a big dance floor to gyrate on. International guest DJs keep the sounds fresh.
☎ 012 429 69 83 🖳 www.klubmidgard.pl ✉ Szpitalna 38 € varies ⌚ 6pm-1am Sun-Wed, 6pm-3am Thu-Sat 🚋 2, 3, 4, 5, 13, 24

Stalowe Magnolie (4, C2)
One of Kraków's most fashionable clubs, this is a great place to enjoy a varied programme of live music, including jazz, rock and salsa. Dress smartly and ring the doorbell.
☎ 012 422 84 72 🖳 www.stalowemagnolie.com ✉ Św Jana 15 € varies ⌚ 6pm-3am, music from 9pm

TEA & COFFEE HOUSES

Bar 13 (2, B3)
In the basement of the Pasaż Handlowy Rynek 13 shopping centre, Bar 13 is a stylish little coffee bar frequented by local office workers. It also serves wine and tapas, and day-old English newspapers and magazines are provided for customers.
☎ 012 617 02 27 ✉ Rynek Główny 13 ⌚ 9am-7pm

Coffee Republic (2, A3)
Popular with the student crowd, this is a laid-back place to linger over a coffee, though the 'designer' seating is almost as uncomfortable as it looks. You can borrow board games if you want to settle down for an hour or two.
☎ 0605 40 33 82 ✉ Bracka 4 ⌚ 8.30am-midnight ♿ fair 🚻

Demmers Teehaus (4, C6)
Take a break from sightseeing and sip Darjeeling, sencha green tea or a host of other black, green or herbal teas in the medieval cellar of this Viennese tea house. A shop upstairs sells packaged leaf tea.
☎ 012 423 16 60 🖳 www.herbaciarnia.com.pl ✉ Kanonicza 21 ⌚ 11am-7pm

Friends Coffee (4, A2)
One of Kraków's longer-opening coffee bars, Friends is, as the name suggests, a welcoming little caffeine pit stop, with soft sofas, magazines and a good range of cakes. It's also quieter and more relaxed than the more central bars.

TriBeCa is a warm and inviting coffee spot

🖥 www.coffeefriends.pl
✉ Karmelicka 14 🕑 7am-10pm Mon-Fri, 8am-10pm Sat, 9am-9pm Sun 🚊 4, 8, 13, 14, 24

Pożegnanie z Afryką (2, C1)

'Out of Africa' offers rare coffees such as Jamaican Blue Mountain, Hawaiian Kona and Yemen Matari in various forms, from espressos to cappuccinos. They also sell packaged coffee and a unique range of jewellery made with silvered coffee beans.
☎ 012 644 47 45 ✉ Św Tomasza 21 🕑 10am-7pm Mon-Fri, 10am-5pm Sat & Sun 🚻 fair (entry on Floriańska)

TriBeCa Coffee (2, A2)

Always busy, TriBeCa is a convenient spot for a caffè latte or a quick snack. Lounge on squashy sofas in the front, or sit up at a table in the back, if you can get one. There's outdoor seating on the square in good weather.
☎ 012 423 03 44 ✉ Rynek Główny 27 🕑 9am-9pm 🚻 good (outdoor tables)

Wiśniowy Sad (4, C5)

With its antiques and froufrou furnishings, the 'Cherry Orchard' evokes the lacy world of a Chekov play. Russian-style tea and pastries are offered, and there are occasional piano recitals. Invite a maiden aunt along.
☎ 012 430 21 11
✉ Grodzka 33
🕑 10am-10pm

CLASSICAL MUSIC, OPERA & THEATRE

Filharmonia Krakowska (4, A5)

The Kraków Philharmonic is one of Poland's finest orchestras, and leading international acts also perform in the grand concert hall. Violinist Nigel Kennedy is visiting artistic director of this venerable institution.
☎ 012 422 94 77 🖥 www.filharmonia.krakow.pl
✉ Zwierzyniecka € 10-60zł 🕑 box office noon-7pm Tue-Fri & 1hr before concerts Sat & Sun 🚊 1, 2, 6, 7, 8

Kabaret Loch Camelot (2, C1)

One of the most popular of Kraków's legendary cabarets, Loch Camelot plays in the cellar of Café Camelot. Expect a riotous mixture of music, satire, poetry and comedy, all in Polish of course. 'Audience participation', willing or otherwise, is also on the cards.
☎ 012 421 01 23 🖥 www.lochcamelot.art.pl
✉ Św Tomasza 17 € 29zł 🕑 shows Fri around 8pm

Słowacki Theatre (4, E2)

Built in 1893 and modelled on the Paris Opéra, this elegant theatre hosts a regular programme of operatic standards and

---

SOLO TRAVELLERS

Entertaining your solitary self in Kraków is easy. Cafés and pubs are commonly frequented by lone locals and foreign visitors alike, enjoying their own company with a newspaper, good book, or just a good beer. Similarly, you won't feel out of place in live music venues, which often have many single attendees.

If you'd rather have a more sociable time at one of the city's many beer halls, head for one of the less crowded benches and ask *Czy to miejsce jest wolne?* (Is this seat free?) before sitting down. You might even make some new friends.

SPECIAL EVENTS

February *Shanties International Sailor Song Festival* – ship-shape fun at the Rotunda Cultural Centre

May *Kraków Film Festival* – founded in 1961, one of Europe's oldest international movie festivals. Various locations

Dragon's Parade – Puppetry, music and street theatre celebrating the Wawel Dragon, at Rynek Główny, Błonia and river bank beneath Wawel Hill

June *Lajkonik* – the famous Kraków hobby horse is celebrated with an historical pageant on Rynek Główny

July *Jewish Cultural Festival* – early July; huge festival of Jewish music and culture, held at various locations in Kazimierz

Summer Jazz Festival – throughout July, international jazz acts perform at Pod Baranami

September *Sacrum-Profanum Festival*, mid-late September; themed classical concerts at the Filharmonia and other venues

October *Organ Music Festival* – a celebration of organ compositions at the Filharmonia

November *Festival of Polish Music* – early November; Polish and international artists perform classic Polish music at the Filharmonia and in various churches

Christmas Fair – late November and December; local arts and crafts for sale on Rynek Główny

December *Szopki Competition* – early December; local artists compete to make Kraków's most beautiful Nativity scene, displayed on Rynek Główny (see p50)

theatrical performances. The interior, dripping with stucco, marble and murals, is breathtaking. Advance bookings are essential. ☎ 012 421 16 30 🖳 www. slowacki.krakow.pl ✉ Św Ducha 1 € 22-55zł 🕥 box office 10am-1pm & 4-7pm Mon, Fri & Sat, 1-6pm Tue, Wed & Thu, noon-7pm Sun 🚊 2, 3, 4, 5, 13, 14

Stary Teatr (4, B3)
Kraków's esteemed 'Old Theatre' is famous throughout the country for the quality of its productions.

It presents a wide repertoire of both classic Polish and foreign plays; all shows are in Polish.

☎ 012 422 40 40 🖳 www. stary-teatr.pl ✉ Jagiellońska 1 € 30-50zł; discounts available for children 🕥 box office 10am-1pm & 5-7pm Tue-Sat

Teatr Bagatela (4, A2)
Bagatela is one of the city's leading venues for drama, staging plays by both Polish and foreign writers, although all performances are in Polish. Recent productions include versions of Tennessee Williams' *The Glass Menagerie*, and *The Secret Garden* by Frances Hodgson Burnett.

☎ 012 422 66 77 🖳 www. bagatela.pl ✉ Karmelicka 6 € 15-49zł; discounts available for children 🕥 box office 9am-7.15pm, shows 7.15pm 🚊 4, 8, 13, 14, 24

Teatr Groteska (3, C4)
The 'Grotesque Theatre' is known for its creepy wordless puppet shows based on old tales and legends. Cabaret, music and a variety of other slightly quirky performances are also on the playbill.

☎ 012 633 48 22 🖳 www. groteska.pl ✉ Skarbowa 2 € 13-25zł 🕥 box office 8am-noon & 3-5pm, shows around 8pm 🚌 103, 113, 164, 179 ♿

Wooden puppets at the Teatr Groteska

JAZZ

Art Club Cieplarnia (4, B4)

During the day, Cieplarnia is an attractive little restaurant serving a mix of Polish and Swiss cuisine. In the evenings of Thursday, Friday and Saturday, an equally eclectic mix of jazz and poetry readings is staged.

☎ 012 429 28 98 ✉ Bracka 15 € vary ☾ 10am-11pm, shows Thu-Sat from 8pm

Harris Piano Jazz Bar (2, A2)

Yet another smoky, subterranean jazz haunt, Harris has one of Kraków's most varied programmes. Shows usually take place Thursday to Saturday, with occasional performances at other times. Jam sessions are on Thursday while Friday is given over to the blues.

☎ 012 421 57 41 ▱ www.harris.krakow.pl ✉ Rynek Główny 28 € 20-30zł ☾ 10am-2am

Jazz Club U Muniaka (2, C2)

Regarded by many as Kraków's pre-eminent jazz venue, this subterranean club was founded by the saxophonist Janusz Muniak. It attracts an impressive roll call of international artists, and is regularly packed out with both tourist and local aficionados.

☎ 012 423 12 05 ▱ www.umuniaka.krakow.pl ✉ Floriańska 3 € 20-40zł ☾ 6.30pm-2am

Indigo Jazz Club (4, D2)

Positioned in amazing vaulted cellars with great acoustics, Indigo attracts a slightly more middle-aged crowd with its top-class jazz. There's no strict concert schedule, but a range of acts from Poland and overseas plays here on two or three evenings a week.

☎ 012 421 48 65 ✉ Floriańska 26 € varies ☾ 3pm-3am

Piec' Art (4, B3)

This cosy cellar club stages some top-class jazz acts from Poland and elsewhere and it always attracts a crowd at weekends.

☎ 012 429 64 25 ▱ www.piccart.onet.pl ✉ Szewska 12 € 35-40zł ☾ 11am-midnight Sun-Thu, 11am-1am Fri & Sat 🚊 2, 7, 8, 14, 15

CINEMAS

ARS Cinema (2, B1)

This small cinema in the centre of town shows a variety of new films from the US and Europe, most screened in the original language, with Polish subtitles. There's an Internet café on site.

☎ 012 421 41 99 ▱ www.dokina.pl ✉ Św Jana 6 € 10-15zł; discounts available for children ☾ 11am-11pm

Cinema City (3, D5)

Inside Galeria Kazimierz (p26), the Cinema City multiplex has ten screens showing the latest Hollywood releases, as well as European films. Most are shown in the original language, with Polish subtitles.

☎ 012 254 54 54 ▱ www.cinema-city.pl ✉ Galeria Kazimierz, Podgórska 34, Kazimierz € 16/13zł; discounts available for children ☾ 10am-midnight 🚊 3, 9, 11, 13, 24 🅿

A top venue in Kraków's lively jazz scene

Kino Pod Baranami (2, A2)

The Pod Baranami cinema shows a wide variety of nearly new and much older 'classic' European films. Foreign films are shown in the original language, usually with Polish subtitles, though not always.
☎ 012 423 07 68 ⊠ Rynek Główny 27 € 14/10zł; discounts available for children ⏱ 11am-11pm

GAY & LESBIAN KRAKÓW

7 Club (3, D3)

The 7 Club offers a diverse programme of music, films and drag shows during the week, and discos Friday and Saturday. It's a discreet place, and operates a door selection policy.
☎ 012 631 95 00
🖥 www.7klub.com ⊠ Św Filipa 7, Kleparz € 5zł Fri & Sat, free Sun-Thu ⏱ 6pm-2am Sun-Thu, 6pm-5am Fri & Sat 🚊 3, 5, 7, 19

Club A'tak (4, B3)

One of Kraków's latest gay establishments, A'tak is a two-level club with a couple of dance floors and bars. It's popular with the young student crowd, and there are occasional concerts and other events, for which there is a charge.
☎ 012 632 22 96
⊠ Plac Szczepanski 2
€ free ⏱ pub 11am-1am, discos 9pm-5am Thu-Sun
🚊 2, 4, 7, 13, 14, 24 🅿

Kitsch (4, E5)

Kraków's most popular gay club, Kitsch is a flamboyant

LAJKONIK

Resembling a gaudy pantomime prop, the Lajkonik is a Kraków tradition stretching back two centuries or so. The fantastical figure is a man, dressed as a Tatar warrior, 'riding' a toy horse worn around his waist; the spangly costume was designed by the ubiquitous Stanisław Wyspiański in 1904. In June, officially on a Thursday seven days after Corpus Christi, the Lajkonik heads a colourful procession, accompanied with music, from the suburb of Zwierzyniec to Rynek Główny. Along the way he dances, collects donations and taps onlookers with his mace for good luck. At the main square, he is greeted by the mayor with a glass of wine. It supposedly commemorates an event from the times of the Tatar invasions in the 13th century, but the facts are vague. Basically it's just an excuse for some unruly fun.

place full of arty décor and camp, over-the-top furnishings. The discos and parties attract a mixed crowd of young locals and visitors.

☎ 012 422 52 99 🖥 www.kitsch.pl ⊠ 3rd floor, Wielopole 15 € ⏱ 7pm-4am Sun-Thu, 8pm-6am Fri & Sat 🚌 607, 609

Sleeping

Kraków is Poland's top tourist destination, so there's no shortage of places to stay. Inevitably, though, prices tend to be above the Polish average, and advance bookings are advisable during the busy Easter, summer and Christmas seasons. The Old Town (Stare Miasto) is the main place to find deluxe and top-end hotels, as well as several very good midrange establishments. Do note, though, that late-opening bars and clubs mean that noise can be a problem if you have a room overlooking busy pedestrian streets. Kazimierz is a quieter option, offering several small, attractive hotels, some with a Jewish ambience.

Real budget accommodation is mainly the preserve of hostels, which tend to be further out. However, recent years have seen several smart new hostels opening in more central locations, and these have proved very popular. Another recent trend has been the growth of self-contained apartments, which are ideal if you intend staying for more than a few days.

ROOM RATES

The categories indicate the cost per night of a standard double room in high season, and the cost per night for a bed in budget accommodation

Deluxe	over 650zł
Top End	351–650zł
Midrange	101–350zł
Budget	up to 100zł

DELUXE

Grand Hotel (4, C2)
This former ducal palace opened as a hotel in 1887, and today has 62 rooms and nine individually designed suites. The largest, with Empire-style furnishings and pink marble, is especially grand. Joseph Conrad and Margaret Thatcher are among the past guests.
☎ 012 421 72 55 ▯ www.grand.pl ✉ Sławkowska 5 ♿ good (barrier-free rooms) ✗ Mirror Hall Restaurant

Hotel Copernicus (4, C6)
On one of Kraków's most picturesque cobbled streets, just a few steps from Wawel Hill, Copernicus is among the city's finest hotels. Wood-beamed ceilings and marble bathrooms make for a sumptuous atmosphere.
☎ 012 424 34 00 ▯ www.

hotel.com.pl ✉ Kanonicza 16 🚌 103, 502 ♿ good ♿ ✗ Copernicus (p33)

Hotel Pod Różą (2, C1)
'Under the Roses' is a classic old Kraków hotel that has hosted European royalty and the likes of Franz Liszt over the years. Rooms are large and furnished with antiques, and there's an excellent restaurant.
☎ 012 424 33 00 ▯ www.hotel.com.pl ✉ Floriańska 14 ✗

TOP END

Hotel Amadeus (4, D3)
With its Mozartian flair, Amadeus is a refined place with some 20 tastefully furnished rooms. They do vary in size, though, and some singles are a little small. There's a well-regarded gourmet restaurant on site.
☎ 012 429 60 70 ▯ www.hotel-amadeus.pl ✉ Mikołajska 20 🚌 3, 10, 13, 19, 24 ♿ fair ✗ Amadeus

The elegant courtyard of the Hotel Copernicus

Ostoya Palace Hotel (3, C4)

The 24 rooms in this elegant 19th-century palace combine old-world furnishings with all the mod-cons you could wish for, including broadband Internet, satellite TV, and underfloor heating in the bathrooms. It also has its own restaurant.

☎ 012 430 90 00
🖳 www.ostoyapalace.pl
✉ Piłsudskiego 24, Nowy Świat 🚊 15, 18
Ⓟ ♿ good 🗶

Wentzl (2, A3)

In a medieval building known as the 'town house under the painting', after the huge icon of the Virgin on the façade, Wentzl has 12 spacious rooms with wood-beamed ceilings and plush furnishings. One of Kraków's better restaurants is downstairs.

☎ 012 430 26 64 🖳 www. wentzl.pl ✉ Rynek Główny 19 🗶 Wentzl

MIDRANGE

Hotel Eden (6, C2)

Occupying three restored 15th-century houses, Eden has 27 simple but comfortable rooms of varying sizes, and Poland's only working *mikveh*, or Jewish ritual bathhouse. There's also a sauna and mini-spa with therapeutic salt treatments, and a cellar pub, Ye Olde Goat.

☎ 012 430 65 65 🖳 www. hoteleden.pl ✉ Ciemna 15, Kazimierz 🚊 3, 9, 11, 13, 24 ♿ good Ⓟ 🗶 Eden

Hotel Royal (6, A1)

This huge 19th-century hotel right opposite Wawel Hill is split into two sections. The more expensive two-star rooms, with shining modern bathrooms, are better value than the rather drab one-star rooms at the back.

☎ 012 421 35 00 🖳 www. royal.com.pl ✉ Św Gertrudy 26-29 🚊 6, 8, 10, 18 Ⓟ 🗶

Hotel Klezmer Hois (6, C2)

This quaint old place – a former *mikveh* (Jewish bathhouse) – is an evocative slice of old Kazimierz. There are just 10 rooms, furnished with antiques and Jewish artworks. There's an art gallery in the cellar, and the restaurant features live music nightly.

☎ 012 411 12 45 🖳 www. klezmer.pl ✉ Szeroka 6, Kazimierz 🚊 3, 9, 11, 13, 24 🗶 Klezmer Hois (p35)

Hotel Petrus (3, B5)

Escape the crowds at this beautifully appointed hotel close to the dramatic Park Skały Twardowskiego, around 2km southwest of the city centre. Rooms are cool and modern and there's a cosy lounge with a log fire, and a sauna.

☎ 012 269 29 46 🖳 www. petrus.net.pl ✉ Pietrusińskiego 12, Dębniki 🚌 100, 112, 162 Ⓟ 🗶 Petrus

Hotel Saski (2, B1)

The historic Saski, with its liveried doorman and rattling century-old lift, offers a touch of fin-de-siècle ambience at reasonable rates. Rooms are relatively plain, but the breakfast in the adjoining Metropolitan restaurant is possibly the best in town.

Don't worry, the Hotel Royal has a lift too...

☎ 012 421 42 22
🖳 www.hotelsaski.com.pl
✉ Sławkowska 3
🗶 Metropolitan (p32)

Hotel Wit Stwosz (4, E3)

This renovated 16th-century town house belongs to St Mary's Church, hence all the Bibles and crucifixes in the rooms. It's a quiet, relaxing place and a bargain for this central location.

☎ 012 429 60 26 🖳 www. wit-stwosz.com.pl
✉ Mikołajska 28 🚊 3, 10, 13 🗶 Bombaj Tandoori (p31)

Old Town Square B&B (2, A1)

Run by Old Town Apartments (see box, p46), this modern B&B just off the main square offers neat little rooms with kitchenettes and private bathrooms. There's also a laundry room, and breakfast is included.

☎ 012 421 42 01
🖳 www.bb-krakow.com
✉ Szczepańska 3
🗶 Pod Ogródkiem (p33)

Wielopole Guest Rooms
(4, E5)

This bright and friendly place in a renovated block just east of the Old Town has modern, unfussy rooms with spotless bathrooms. Breakfast, served in your room, costs extra.

☎ 012 422 14 75 ▯ www. wielopole.pl ✉ Wielopole 3 🚃 3, 13 🚌 607, 609 Ⓟ ✕ Bar Vega (p33)

BUDGET

Bursa Jagiellońska
(3, D6)

This university hostel offers basic singles, doubles and triples from July to September only (i.e. outside term time). It's a little out of the way, but the on-site facilities, including kitchens, free laundry and Internet, amply make up for that. Breakfast, lunch and dinner available at extra cost.

☎ 012 656 12 66 ▯ www. bursa.krakow.pl ✉ Śliska 14, Podgórze 🚃 10 Ⓟ ✕

Cracow Hostel (2, A1)
The location of this modern hostel, overlooking the main

Hotel Amadeus (p44) offers good service and gourmet food

square, is unbeatable. Dorm rooms are bright and clean, and there's a communal kitchen, lounge and laundry, and Internet access. The price includes breakfast and linen.

☎ 012 429 11 06 ▯ www. cracowhostel.com ✉ Rynek Główny 18 ✕ Sioux (p30)

Gardenhouse Hostel
(2, C2)

This smart hostel in the shadow of St Mary's Church has light, airy dorms with between two and six bunks. Breakfast, Internet access, laundry and bike hire are all

free, and there's a secluded garden too.

☎ 012 431 28 24 ▯ www.gardenhouse.pl ✉ Floriańska 5 🚃 3, 10, 13, 19 ✕ Green Way (p31)

Momotown Hostel
(6, C1)

Opened in 2005, Momotown is an inviting modern hostel on the edge of Kazimierz, with large clean dorms and sparkling bathrooms. They offer free airport and train station pickups, and every fourth night is free.

☎ 012 429 69 29 ▯ www. momotownhostel.com ✉ Miodowa 28, Kazimierz 🚃 3, 9, 11, 13, 24 ✕ Arka Noego (p35)

Nathan's Villa (6, A2)
Nathan's, conveniently placed halfway between the Old Town and Kazimierz, has brightly painted dorms and a friendly atmosphere. It offers free breakfast, laundry and Internet access, and a pub in the cellar.

☎ 012 422 35 45 ▯ www.nathansvilla.com ✉ Św Agnieszki 1, Stradom 🚃 6, 8, 10 ✕ Kuchnia i Wino

APARTMENTS

If you intend staying in Kraków for more than just a few days, or if you prefer more independence, then you might find a self-contained apartment works out more convenient – and cheaper – than a hotel.

Old Town Apartments (2, A1; ☎ 012 421 42 01; www.warsawshotel.com; ✉ Szczepańska 3) has centrally located apartments with kitchens from €50 per night; Sodispar Service Apartments (3, C2; ☎ 0602 247 438; www.sodispar.pl; ✉ Lubelska 12) offers a range of apartments with private bathrooms and kitchens, from 100zł; and Finger Guest Rooms (3, D3; ☎ 012 423 40 16; ✉ Warszawska 18) has doubles with kitchenettes for 120zł.

About Kraków

HISTORY
Early Years

A permanent settlement in Kraków was established in the 7th century AD by the Slavic Wiślanie tribe. The earliest written record of the nascent town dates from 965, when a Jewish merchant from Cordoba called Ibrahim ibn Yaqub visited, and referred to it as Krakwa. The first recorded ruler of 'Wielkopolska' (Great Poland), which included Kraków, was Mieszko I. He converted to Christianity in 966, making his kingdom part of Christian Europe, and in 1000 an archbishopric was founded in Kraków.

The turrets of the Barbican (p19)

Middle Ages

In 1038 Kazimierz I moved his capital from Gniezno to Kraków, and Wawel Castle was begun. After Kraków was burned to the ground by the Tatars in 1241, an ambitious reconstruction began. The new town centre was laid out in 1257 with a great market square at its centre, the layout that remains today. The city experienced a 'Golden Age' under the enlightened rule of Kazimierz Wielki ('the Great') in the 14th century. He founded the Kraków Academy, later renamed the Jagiellonian University, and the new town of Kazimierz. By the 15th century, a combination of astute dynastic marriages and military successes made the Polish state the largest in Europe.

Renaissance to Communism

Kraków in the 16th century was a wealthy and cultured city. Arts and sciences flourished and the city's population, estimated at around 30,000, was a cosmopolitan mix of nationalities and religions, co-existing in relative harmony. However, in 1595 it was decided to move the capital to Warsaw. Kings were still crowned and buried in Kraków's Cathedral but the city's political importance faded.

Surrounded by three powerful expansionist empires, Poland was ripe for the picking when, in 1773, Russia, Prussia and Austria decided to divide the country up between them; a process that was completed in 1795 when Poland was wiped from the map. Kraków found itself inside the Austrian Empire, where it remained until 1918.

The Nazis marched into Poland in 1939 and mass arrests, killings and looting ensued in Kraków. Jews were deported to the gas chambers of Auschwitz. The city was finally liberated in January 1945, and a communist government imposed by the Soviets. In 1949 the authorities began construction of the Nowa Huta steelworks east of the city centre, a

Setting the world to rights at an outdoor art gallery in Old Town

move designed to break the city's suspiciously 'bourgeois' culture. Instead, it brought acid rain and smog.

The election of Karol Wojtyła, Kraków's archbishop, to the papacy in 1978 – when he took the name Pope John Paul II – gave a boost to the anti-communist movement across Poland. In 1989 the communist regime collapsed, and in 1990 Lech Wałęsa was elected president.

NATO to EU

Political instability and social problems caused by the new free-market reforms characterised much of the 1990s. Former Communist Aleksander Kwasniewski won the presidential election in 1995, but Poland continued to orient itself towards the West, joining NATO in 1999 and the EU in 2004. In 2005 Lech Kaczynski of the Law and Justice Party (PiS) was elected president. His call for a return to traditional Catholic values drew much support in Kraków.

ENVIRONMENT

Although the antiquated Nowa Huta steelworks (p19) have been upgraded in recent years, they remain a source of air pollution in Kraków, as do factories in the industrial heartland of Silesia to the west of the city. Smog is a common feature during the cold

DID YOU KNOW?
- Population 800,000
- Inflation 3.5%
- Unemployment 5%
- Average Polish monthly wage 2100zł
- Average price of pub beer 5zł/500ml

winter months as many residents still use cheap coal to heat their homes. The River Wisła suffers from pollution too, coming from industrial emissions up and down stream, although this doesn't seem to deter the odd fisherman from waving his rod about along the banks.

Recycling is a feature of domestic life in Kraków and you'll see plenty of recycling bins for various materials in residential areas.

ECONOMY

Kraków is Poland's biggest tourist draw by a wide margin, and tourism is of prime importance to the city's economy. It is also Poland's fourth-largest manufacturing centre, with steelmaking and pharmaceuticals being the main industries, while the city's 15 institutions of higher education are big employers in themselves. The average unemployment rate in Poland hovers around 20%, but Kraków fares rather better, with an unemployment rate of just 5%, due in no small part to the large graduate population in the city. Inward investment is growing too. The ambitious 'Nowe Miasto' development around the train station, which is to include a huge shopping centre, multiplex, restaurants and a 4-star hotel, is due for completion by the end of 2006, though work is progressing slowly.

SOCIETY & CULTURE

Kraków is Poland's third-largest city, with Poles making up around 98% of the population, and the remaining 2% consisting of a varied assortment of other European nationalities. There are around 100,000 university students in Kraków, and numerous monastic communities, while the rough-edged suburb of Nowa Huta, with its social problems, is a real contrast.

Poles are a generally friendly and hospitable people, but tend to be much more conservative and traditional than Westerners. This is especially apparent in Kraków, with its strong religious traditions, and in every church you will see people kneeling in prayer. However, walk into any pub and you'll see a less sober side to Kraków life, as locals joyfully let their hair down over several beers.

Etiquette

If attending more highbrow cultural events such as classical concerts or opera, smart casual is the preferred style, though attitudes are a lot more relaxed if you're heading for a smoky jazz cellar. Many clubs in Kraków operate a very strict door selection policy, and locals dress to impress (even if this does mean looking like Barbie).

Public drunkenness isn't uncommon, but it is frowned upon, not least by the police. Smoking is very common, everywhere, although it is normal to refrain during lunch.

National poet Adam Mickiewicz (p51)

ARTS
Architecture

The earliest architectural style you'll see in Kraków is Romanesque, best exemplified by the severe Church of St Andrew (p18), although its interior received a baroque makeover in the 18th century.

Gothic architecture is much better represented in Kraków, and is characterised by high pointed arches and ribbed vaults. St Mary's Church (p11), Wawel Cathedral (p9) and the Collegium Maius (p15) are among the chief Gothic structures in Kraków.

The 16th century ushered in a new style, loosely termed 'Renaissance', which paid much attention to decorative details. The grand interiors of Wawel Castle are good examples. Baroque, the exuberant and lavish style which flourished in the 17th and 18th centuries, was favoured by many of Kraków's churches, including the Church of SS Peter and Paul (p18).

The 19th century saw a revival of older styles such as neo-Gothic, while art nouveau took off towards the end of the century. Its influence can be seen in the Queen Zofia Chapel in Wawel Cathedral and in domestic architecture like the House under the Spider (p21).

The monolithic socialist realism style employed by the Soviets found one of its greatest expressions in the 1950s suburb of Nowa Huta, though Kraków's Old Town thankfully escaped the communist concrete treatment.

Painting & Sculpture

Kraków has an artistic tradition dating back several centuries, but the 19th century saw its most prolific painters at work. The city's most lauded artist was Jan Matejko, who specialised in vast, dramatic scenes of key moments in Polish history which proved hugely popular at a time of growing national consciousness.

KRAKÓW'S CRIBS

Walk into Rynek Główny in the first week of December and all around the statue of Adam Mickiewicz you'll see a host of glittering Nativity scenes, called *Szopki*, laid out for judging in the annual competition. Made with great care and imagination by local artists, these highly detailed creations all employ architectural elements from Kraków landmarks – the spires of St Mary's Church are a favourite motif – and are peopled with little figures representing characters from the city's history or current politics and often powered by clockwork mechanisms. The actual Nativity scene itself is but a small part of these elaborate *Szopki*, which are made to be as colourful as possible. The competition dates from only 1937. Winners have their Nativity scenes displayed in the Historical Museum until February.

Head to Rynek Główny (p10) to see Igor Mitoraj's two-tonne bronze

The Young Poland (Młoda Polska) movement, which developed in Kraków around the turn of the 19th and 20th centuries, fused elements of art nouveau with Impressionism and national Romanticism. One of the movement's leading figures was Stanisław Wyspiański, whose creations include the flowery murals and stained-glass windows in the Franciscan Church (p19). Jacek Malczewski was a leading exponent of Symbolism, while Józef Chełmoński was a more traditional artist. Works of both artists hang in the Cloth Hall.

Literature

Polish poetry and literature blossomed in the 19th century. The poets Adam Mickiewicz and Juliusz Słowacki are regarded as national icons, while the ever-busy Stanisław Wyspiański also turned his hand to playwriting, producing the much admired *Wesele* (The Wedding).

Stanisław Lem is Poland's best-known science fiction writer, while two Kraków-based poets, Czesław Miłosz and Wisława Szymborska, each won more international recognition when they received the Nobel Prize for Literature, in 1980 and 1996 respectively.

Music

Famous Kraków composers include Krzysztof Penderecki, who produced dramatic orchestral pieces such as *Dies Irae* and *Devils of Loudun*, and Zbigniew Preisner, best known for his award-winning film scores.

Kraków has the liveliest jazz scene in Poland after Warsaw, and its clubs attract performers from across the world. Klezmer music (Jewish music based on Eastern European folk songs) too has won large audiences. The top local combo are the *Klezmatics*, while former member and clarinet virtuoso David Krakauer now leads his own band, *Klezmer Madness*.

Another klezmer/folk act, the *Kroke Band*, recorded an internationally successful album, *East meets East*, in 2003, with British violinist Nigel Kennedy. He is also visiting artistic director of the Kraków Philharmonic.

ARRIVAL & DEPARTURE
Air
Kraków's **Balice Airport** (3, off A2; Medweckiego 1, Balice; www.lotinsko-balice.pl), also known as John Paul II International Airport, is 12km west of the city centre, to which it is connected with regular bus services. It's a small airport, where facilities include a bar and restaurant, information desks, car rental agencies, accommodation agencies, bank, post office and money exchange offices.

INFORMATION
General Enquiries (24hr)
☎ 012 285 51 20
Car Park Information ☎ 012 258 77 00

Flight Information
Air France ☎ 022 846 03 03
British Airways ☎ 012 285 50 33
easyJet ☎ 012 639 34 28
LOT Polish Airlines ☎ 012 639 31 33
Lufthansa ☎ 0801 312 312

AIRPORT ACCESS
Bus
Bus X08 (4zł) runs between the airport and the Filharmonia stop on Straszewskiego, roughly 250m southwest of Rynek Główny. Alternatively, catch the more frequent bus 192 from Plac Matejki, 208 from Nowy Kleparz (both 2.50zł) or the private Radtur shuttle bus from the main bus station on Bosacka (7zł). The trip takes about 30–40 minutes by bus.

Taxi
Radio Taxi (☎ 9191) is the only official company with a dedicated rank at the airport. A taxi to the city centre should cost no more than 60zł.

Bus
International and some regional services operated by the state bus company **PKS** (☎ 012 411 70 22; www.pks.krakow.pl)

run from the modern Regionaly Dworzec Autobusowy station on Bosacka (3, D3). At the time of writing, most domestic services were using a bus station at Cystersów 15 (3, E3). This will continue until the Nowe Miasto development around Plac Kolejowy is completed during 2006.

Train
Polish State Railways (PKP) run inexpensive and reliable services to cities across Poland from Kraków's **main train station**, Kraków Główny (4, F1; Plac Kolejowy). It's also a major hub for international services.
Domestic connections information
☎ 012 422 41 82
International connections information
☎ 012 422 22 48

Travel Documents
VISA
UK citizens can remain in Poland without need of a visa for up to six months. Other EU citizens, as well as nationals of Australia, Canada, New Zealand and the USA, are allowed to stay visa-free for up to three months. Citizens of other countries should contact their nearest Polish embassy or consulate for current regulations before they travel, as visas cannot be issued at the Polish border.

Customs & Duty Free
If travelling within the EU, visitors can import or export 90L of wine, 110L of beer, 10L of spirits and 200 cigarettes before having to pay duty. Note that anything made before 1945 is classified as an antique and cannot be exported without an export permit *(pozwolenie eksportowe)*.

Left Luggage
There are coin-operated left luggage lockers in both the train and bus stations. Small lockers cost 4zł for 24 hours, big lockers cost 8zł.

GETTING AROUND

Kraków's public transport system consists of trams and buses run by the **municipal transport company, MPK** (☎ 9150; www.mpk.krakow.pl). Apart from the tram lines which run east–west across Dominikańska and Franciszkańska, no public transport operates within the Old Town bounded by the Planty. Many visitors will end up walking, as most sites of interest in Kraków are in a pleasingly compact area. In this book, the nearest bus or tram routes are noted after the symbols 🚌 and 🚊 .

Travel Passes

Public transport tickets for 24 hours (10.40zł), 48 hours (18.80zł) and 72 hours (25zł) are available. However, unless you envisage jumping on and off trams and buses several times a day, you will probably find that buying single tickets as and when you need them will be more cost-effective.

Car

As the whole of Kraków's Old Town is either pedestrianised or operates a strictly limited car access and parking system, having your own wheels is likely to be more of a hindrance than a help on a short visit. However, if you need a vehicle, there are a number of rental agencies at Balice Airport (p51), including:
Budget (☎ 012 285 50 25)
Europcar (☎ 012 285 50 45)
Hertz (☎ 012 285 50 84)

Tram & Bus

Public transport operates from 5am to 11pm, with some night buses continuing to run after that time. Single tickets (2.50zł), valid on both trams and buses, can be bought at newsstands. A 1-hour ticket (3.10zł) allows travel with unlimited changes. Both tickets can be bought from the driver, but will cost 50gr more. Remember to validate your ticket in the machines when you board; spot-checks are frequent, and you will be fined 100zł if you do not have a validated ticket. You will need an extra single ticket for large items of luggage (officially those measuring 60cm × 40cm × 20cm or more) unless you are using a travel pass.

The numbers allocated to tram lines have either one or two digits, while bus lines are indicated with three digits. Night buses have three-digit numbers beginning with 6, and a 'night ticket' (5zł) is required for travelling on these services.

Taxi

Most taxi-drivers in Kraków are above board and use their meters, but there are plenty of dishonest drivers around, especially outside the train station and airport. Genuine, licensed cabs will have a sign on the roof and the name of the company, with its phone number, prominently displayed. Do not get into an unmarked car, and do not accept a lift from drivers who might approach you touting for business. Only use official ranks, or call reliable taxi firms such as: **Barbakan Taxi** (☎ 9661); **Express Taxi** (☎ 0800 111 111); **Metro Taxi** (☎ 9667); **Radio Taxi** (☎ 9191).

PRACTICALITIES
Climate & When to Go

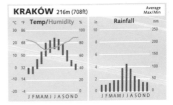

Kraków attracts visitors year-round, with the largest numbers between June and August, and at Easter and Christmas. Late spring, before too many visitors have arrived, and summer are the best times for exploring the city. The city looks very picturesque under a covering of winter snow, and accommodation is plentiful at this time, but it can be very cold and susceptible to smog. Most attractions will either be closed or operating with restricted opening hours between November and March.

Consulates

France (4, C4; Stolarska 15; ☎ 012 424 53 00)

Germany (2, C3; Stolarska 7; ☎ 012 424 30 00)

UK (4, B3; Św Anny 9; ☎ 012 421 70 30)

USA (2, C3; Stolarska 9; ☎ 012 424 51 00)

Disabled Travellers

With its cobbled lanes and broken and uneven pavements, Kraków can be an awkward place for people in wheelchairs to negotiate. Added to this, many pubs and restaurants tend to be in cellar locations, and public transport is likely to be awkward too. Several museums do now have ramps or lifts for disabled access although these are still in the minority. Sights, restaurants and hotels which provide access for disabled visitors are noted in the relevant reviews.

Discounts

Students with valid international ID cards and children get discounts at most tourist attractions, but not on public transport, unless they are studying in Poland.

If you're planning a packed sightseeing itinerary, then it may be worth getting hold of a **Kraków Card** (www.krakowcard.com), which comes in 2- and 3-day versions (45/65zł). The card, which you can buy at tourist information offices, travel agencies and some hotels, gives free access to around 30 city museums and free use of public transport. Card-holders are also entitled to discounts at some restaurants and shops.

Electricity

Voltage 220v
Frequency 50Hz
Cycle AC
Plugs two round pins

Emergencies

As always, be very wary of pickpockets in places where tourists congregate. Some pickpockets work crowded clubs too.

Car crime has become a big problem in Kraków, so if you do decide to rent a car make sure that you don't leave it in an unguarded area.

Central Kraków is a safe place at night as long as you use your common sense. Areas of the Planty towards the train station are frequented at night by drunks and vagrants who may appear threatening even if they are not actually dangerous.

There have been many reports of robberies on night trains, especially those travelling between Kraków and Germany and the Czech Republic. Criminals have even been known to use a kind of sleeping gas to render passengers unconscious before rifling though their belongings. It's advisable to book a couchette if you intend using these services.

Ambulance ☎ 999
Fire ☎ 998
Police ☎ 997
Police (English/German-language assistance; ☎ 0800 200 300; 8am-8pm)

Gay & Lesbian Travellers

Homosexuality is legal in Poland and the age of consent is 15, the same as for heterosexuals. However, Kraków remains a deeply conservative city, and same-sex couples may encounter hostility.

In 2004, Kraków's first ever 'March for Tolerance', organised by the local gay and lesbian community, ended in chaos as marchers were physically attacked in the city centre by large mobs of 'Christians' and far-right thugs. Because of this, the march was cancelled in 2005.

There are a few gay clubs in Kraków, but no venues catering specifically for lesbians.

For more information, log on to www.cracow.gayguide.net, or try the Polish gay portal www.innastrona.pl.

HEALTH
Precautions
Kraków enjoys a generally good standard of public hygiene, but it does have its problems. The heavily chlorinated tap water has an unpleasant taste, and it's probably best to avoid drinking it. Bottled mineral water is cheap and widely available.

Air pollution is a more serious hazard, coming especially from the antiquated Nowa Huta steelworks in the east, and smog from domestic coal fires in winter.

Smoking is common, and pubs are often filled with dense cigarette fumes. The situation is especially unpleasant in the windowless and unventilated cellars which accommodate many of Kraków's drinking establishments.

Medical Services
EU citizens are covered for most medical care by the European Health Insurance Card (EHIC), but travel insurance is still advisable to cover any medical treatment you may need in Poland. Hospitals and clinics with 24hr accident and emergency care include:
Falck (3, C2; ☎ 9675; Mazowiecka 4)
Medicover (3, D3; ☎ 012 616 10 00; Rakowicka 7)
University Hospital (3, E4; ☎ 012 424 77 30; Śniadekich 10)

DENTAL SERVICES
If you chip a tooth or require emergency treatment, head to **Dent America** (4, B2; ☎ 012 421 89 48; Plac Szczepański 3).

PHARMACIES
The following pharmacies are open 24hr:
Apteka (3, D6; ☎ 012 656 18 50; Kalwaryiska 94)
Apteka (3, C3; ☎ 012 430 00 35; Krowoderska 31)

Holidays
New Year's Day	1 January
Easter Monday	March or April
Labour Day	1 May
Constitution Day	3 May
Corpus Christi	Thursday in May or June
Assumption	15 August
All Saints' Day	1 November
Independence Day	11 November
Christmas Day	25 December
St Stephen's Day	26 December

Internet
There are lots of Internet cafés scattered around Kraków. Connection speeds and prices do vary, and you can expect to pay between roughly 2-4zł per hour.

INTERNET CAFÉS
Internet Klub Garinet (2, C1; ☎ 012 423 22 33; Floriańska 18; ⊙ 9am-12am; 4zł per hour)
Klub Internetowy Labirynt (6, C2; ☎ 012 292 05 14; ✉ Józefa 15, Kazimierz; ⊙ 9am-10pm Mon-Sat, 10am-8pm Sun; 2zł per hour)
Punkt Internetowy (4, C2; ☎ 012 422 22 64; ✉ Sławkowska 12; ⊙ 8am-8pm Mon-Fri; 2zł per hour)

USEFUL WEBSITES
The Lonely Planet website (www.lonelyplanet.com) offers a speedy link to many of Kraków's websites.
Others to try include:
Cracow Life (www.cracow-life.com)
Explore Kraków (www.explore-krakow.com)
Kraków (www.krakow.pl)
Kraków Info (www.krakow-info.com)

Lost Property
Try the **Lost and Found Office** (☎ 012 633 65 26) if you mislay something on public transport.

Metric System
The metric system is used in Poland. Poles use commas rather than decimal points (5,50), and points for thousands (100.000).

Money
CURRENCY
The Polish unit of currency is the złoty, usually contracted to zł, although you will also see PLN used. One złoty is divided into 100 groszy, which are abbreviated to gr. Shops often seem unable to give change for larger denomination banknotes, so try to keep a good supply of coins on you.

TRAVELLERS CHEQUES
Changing travellers cheques in Kraków can be time-consuming and difficult, and few places appear to have the facility to do so. Two places that can change travellers cheques, though, are the *kantor* counters inside the Małopolska Tourist Information Centre (2, B2; Rynek Główny 1) and Orbis Travel (2, B1; Rynek Główny 41).

ATMS
There's no shortage of ATMs in central Kraków, especially around Rynek Główny and neighbouring streets. Most, if not all, banks here have either hole-in-the-wall ATMs or machines indoors. All ATMs accept Visa, MasterCard, Cirrus and Maestro cards.

CHANGING MONEY
You can change money either at one of the big banks, or at a private exchange office, called a *kantor*. These are located all across town, and can be either self-contained offices or just desks in travel agencies and shops, especially souvenir and jewellery shops. You will even find them in some hotels. Be extremely careful when using these places, as some employ rather sneaky tactics to confuse foreigners, such as advertising the rate at which they sell, rather than buy, foreign currencies.

Newspapers & Magazines
The most popular local newspaper is the *Gazetta Krakowska* (www.gk.pl), a daily tabloid available at most newsstands. The best place to find recent copies of

English-language and other international newspapers and magazines is **Empik Megastore** (2, C2; Rynek Główny 5). It also sells *This Month in Kraków* (4zł), a monthly entertainment listings magazine with a brief English summary.

Opening Hours
The following hours are just a guide, and can fluctuate according to the type of business, location and season. Tourist-oriented places are likely to stay open longer, and some open on Sundays.
Shops 9am-6pm Mon-Fri, 10am-3pm Sat
Offices 9am-5pm Mon-Fri
Post Offices 8am-7pm Mon-Fri, 8am-1pm Sat
Restaurants 11am-11pm
Attractions 9am-6pm; many museums and galleries are closed on Mondays

Photography
There are several places in Kraków to get your films processed. There are counters inside **Empik Megastore** (p27) and in the **Galeria Kazimierz** (p26) and **Jubilat** (p26) shopping centres. You could also try **Sonar** (4, C5; cnr Grodzka & Poselska), which sells cameras as well.

Post
Kraków's **main post office** (4, E4; ☎ 012 422 24 97; Westerplatte 20) has an automated queuing system, with dispensing machines issuing tickets. You do not need to take a ticket if you wish to only buy stamps or post a parcel though. Stamps can also be purchased at newsstands.

POSTAL RATES
Standard mail to domestic destinations costs 1.30zł. Postcards and letters to Europe and the rest of the world cost 2.20zł.

Radio
Radio Kraków (101.6 FM) is the main local station, broadcasting the usual mix of music and news programmes.

Telephone

All Kraków phone numbers must be prefaced with the city access code (012), even if calling from within Kraków. Public telephones are commonplace, and phonecards can be purchased at any kiosk or newsstand.

MOBILE PHONES

Poland uses the GSM 900/1800 network, and mobile numbers usually begin with ☎ 05 or ☎ 06. Check with your service provider about using your mobile phone in Poland and beware of calls being routed internationally. You may find buying a Polish SIM card more cost-effective.

Television

Kraków's local TV station is TV3 Kraków, which broadcasts regional news and entertainment programmes. There are two national, state-run TV channels: TV1, which has a light-entertainment format, and TV2, which broadcasts more cultural programmes and documentaries. TVN and Polstat are commercial stations.

Time

Poles use the 24-hour clock. Polish standard time is one hour ahead of GMT and the country observes Daylight Saving Time, putting the clock forward one hour at 2am on the last Sunday in March, and back one hour at 3am on the last Sunday in October.

Tipping

If service at a restaurant has been good, then a tip of 10% is common practice. However, if you say 'thank you', 'ok' or indeed anything else when your waiter collects your money, or even if you nod your head, he may take this to mean that you don't want any change.

Toilets

Public toilets are few and far between in Kraków and those that do exist are not always clean. You will find public toilets at markets, such as the **Cloth Hall** (2, B2) or **Plac Nowy** (6, B2), but it's more pleasant to use toilets at restaurants.

Toilets are labelled '*toaleta*' or simply 'WC' and the gents will usually be marked with a downward-pointing triangle, the ladies with a circle.

Tourist Information

The **Małopolska Tourist Information Centre** (2, B2; ☎ 012 421 77 06; www.mcit.pl; Rynek Główny 1) is the largest of Kraków's three main information points, though apart from a selection of free leaflets (many only in Polish) and brochures, including *The Visitor Małopolska*, it's not particularly helpful.

The smaller **City Tourist Office** (4, E2; ☎ 012 432 01 10; Szpitalna 25) near the main train station can book accommodation for you, while the **tourist office in Kazimierz** (6, B2; ☎ 012 432 08 40; Józefa 7) has the best array of free brochures and the most helpful staff.

In addition, the **Cultural Information Centre** (2, B1; ☎ 012 421 77 87; www.karnet.krakow.pl; Św Jana 2) provides details of, and tickets for, cultural events around town. They sell a monthly programme called *Karnet* (4zł) which has a slim English insert.

Other free monthly brochures worth looking out for include *Welcome to Cracow & Małopolska*, which you can pick up at **Orbis Travel** (2, B1; Rynek Główny 41) and *Krakout* (www.krakoutonline.com), which has some excellent magazine features, as well as listings. You can find it at some hotels.

Women Travellers

Women are unlikely to face any particular problems in Kraków. Lone women entering traditional pubs where macho values and heavy drinking prevail may attract unwelcome attention, but there are plenty of more modern, cosmopolitan bars and coffee houses where they should feel more comfortable.

LANGUAGE

Polish is obviously the main language spoken in Kraków. English and German are widely understood in central Kraków, at least at hotels, restaurants and attractions frequented by foreign tourists. Tram and bus drivers, staff at the train and bus stations and shop workers are less likely to speak anything but Polish. You may find that a copy of Lonely Planet's *Polish Phrasebook* comes in handy.

BASICS

Hello.	Dzień dobry.
Goodbye.	Do widzenia.
Yes.	Tak.
No.	Nie.
Please.	Proszę.
Thank you.	Dziękuję.
You're welcome.	Proszę.
Excuse me.	Przepraszam.
Sorry.	Przepraszam.
My name is ...	Mam na imię ...
I'm from ...	Jestem z ...
I like ...	Lubię ...
I don't like ...	Nie lubię ...

ACCOMMODATION

Where can I find a ...?	Gdzie mogę znaleźć...?
guesthouse	pensjonat
hotel	hotel
youth hostel	schronisko młodzieżowe

What is the address?	Jaki jest adres?
Please write down the address.	Proszę to napisać.

Do you have any rooms available?	Czy są wolne pokoje?

I'd like (a) ...	Poproszę o ...
single room	pokój jednoosobowy
double bed	podwójnym łóżkiem

room	pokój
twin room with two beds	pokój dwuosobowy
room with a bathroom	pokój z łazienką

How much is it per night?	Ile kosztuje za noc?
May I see it?	Czy mogę go zobaczyć?

Where is the bathroom?	Gdzie jest łazienka?
Where is the toilet?	Gdzie są toalety?
I'm leaving today.	Wyjeżdżam dziś.

DIRECTIONS

Where is ...?	Gdzie jest ...?
Go straight ahead.	Proszę iść prosto.
Turn left.	Proszę skręcić w lewo.
Turn right.	Proszę skręcić w prawo.
at the corner	na rogu
at the traffic lights	na światłach

EMERGENCIES

Help!	Na pomoc!
It's an emergency.	To jest nagły przypadek.
I'm lost.	Zgubiłem się. (m) Zgubiłam się. (f)
I'm ill.	Jestem chory/a.
Leave me alone!	Proszę odejść!

Call ...!	Proszę wezwać ...!
a doctor	lekarza
the police	policję

LANGUAGE DIFFICULTIES

Do you speak English?	Czy pan/pani mówi po angielsku? (m/f)
What does it mean?	Co to znaczy?
I understand.	Rozumiem.
I don't understand.	Nie rozumiem.
Could you write it down, please?	Proszę to napisać.

Can you show me (on the map)?	Proszę mi pokazać (na mapie).

NUMBERS

0	zero
1	jeden
2	dwa
3	trzy
4	cztery
5	pięć
6	sześć
7	siedem
8	osiem
9	dziewięć
10	dziesięć
100	sto
1000	tysiąc

SHOPPING & SERVICES

I'd like to buy ...	Chcę kupić ...
How much is it?	Ile to kosztuje?
I don't like it.	Nie podoba mi się.
May I look at it?	Czy mogę to zobaczyć?
I'm just looking.	Tylko oglądam.
It's expensive.	To jest drogie.
I'll take it.	Wezmę to.
Can I pay by credit card?	Czy mogę zapłacić kartą kredytową?
Where's ...?	Gdzie jest ...?
a bank	bank
the bridge	most
the church	kościół
the city centre	centrum
the ... embassy	ambasada ...
the hospital	szpital
the hotel	hotel
an Internet café	kawiarnia internetowa
the market	targ
the museum	muzeum
the police station	posterunek policji
the post office	poczta
a public toilet	toaleta publiczna
the tourist information office	biuro informacji turystycznej

TIME & DATES

What time is it?	Która jest godzina?
It's 10 o'clock.	Jest dziesiąta.
in the morning	rano
in the afternoon	po południu
in the evening	wieczorem
today	dziś/dzisiaj
tomorrow	jutro
yesterday	wczoraj
Monday	poniedziałek
Tuesday	wtorek
Wednesday	środa
Thursday	czwartek
Friday	piątek
Saturday	sobota
Sunday	niedziela

PUBLIC TRANSPORT

What time does the ... leave/arrive?	O której odchodzi/ przychodzi ...?
boat	łódź
bus	autobus
plane	samolot
train	pociąg
tram	tramwaj
I'd like a ... ticket.	Poproszę bilet ...
one-way	w jedną stronę
return	powrotny
I want to go to ...	Chcę jechać do ...
1st class	pierwszą klasę
2nd class	drugą klasę
I'd like to hire a ...	Chcę wypożyczyć ...
bicycle	rower
car	samochód
motorbike	motocykl
Is this the road to ...?	Czy ta droga prowadzi do ...?
Can I park here?	Czy można tu parkować?
How long can I park here?	Jak długo można tu parkować?

Index

See also separate indexes for Eating (p62), Sleeping (p62), Shopping (p62) and Sights with map references (p63).

SIGHTS

FEATURES

🍴 Wierzynek		*Eating*
🎭 Stary Teatr		*Entertainment*
🍸 Boogie		*Drinking*
☕ Friends Coffee		*Café*
🏛 Ethnographical Museum		*Highlights*
🏰 Wawel		*Shopping*
🏛 Historical Museum		*Sights/Activities*
🏨 Grand Hotel		*Sleeping*
● Wieliczka		*Trips & Tours*

AREAS

	Beach, Desert
	Building
	Land
	Mall
	Other Area
	Park/Cemetery
	Sports
	Urban

HYDROGRAPHY

	River, Creek
	Intermittent River
	Canal
	Swamp
	Water

BOUNDARIES

	State, Provincial
	Regional, Suburb

ROUTES

	Tollway
	Freeway
	Primary Road
	Secondary Road
	Tertiary Road
	Lane
	Under Construction
	One-Way Street
	Unsealed Road
	Mall/Steps
	Tunnel
	Walking Path
	Walking Trail/Track
	Pedestrian Overpass
	Walking Tour

TRANSPORT

✈	Airport, Airfield
🚌	Bus Route
🚲	Cycling, Bicycle Path
⛴	Ferry
	General Transport
Ⓜ	Metro
🚝	Monorail
🚆	Rail
🚕	Taxi Rank
🚊	Tram

SYMBOLS

💲	Bank, ATM
🛕	Buddhist
🏰	Castle, Fortress
✝	Christian
🤿	Diving, Snorkeling
⊕	Embassy, Consulate
➕	Hospital, Clinic
@	Information
@	Internet Access
☪	Islamic
✡	Jewish
👁	Lookout
🗿	Monument
▲	Mountain, Volcano
🌲	National Park
Ⓟ	Parking Area
⛽	Petrol Station
🧺	Picnic Area
●	Point of Interest
👮	Police Station
✉	Post Office
🏚	Ruin
🏊	Swimming Pool
☎	Telephone
🚻	Toilets
🦜	Zoo, Bird Sanctuary
💧	Waterfall

24/7 travel advice
www.lonelyplanet.com